Praise for *Lead & Influence*

"Mark has been an influence and inspiration for me over the last decade. He has an extraordinary capability in picking out the important thoughts—putting them in a clear and crisp content—which is then immediately applicable in my daily work."

—**Michael Gabrielsson**
Senior Business Consultant and Partner Mercuri International, Sweden

"In *Lead & Influence*, Mark highlights the mind-sets and habits that help all leaders more effectively influence others ... whether they are located across the hall or across the globe."

—**Waldemar Koper**
Head of Legal SABMiller Poland;
President of Polish Company Lawyers Association seated in Warsaw, Poland

"Mark Fritz's *Lead & Influence* is a powerhouse tome focusing on individual, team, and corporate ownership, commitment, and trust. Chock-full of examples in easy to understand and relatable terms, Mark's work is comprehensive, well-reasoned, and a solid contribution to the art and science of leadership. You should read this book, understand it, and leverage the insights and observations for field use."

—**George M. Beshenich**
Retired Army Colonel;
Resident graduate of the USA War College;
Founder and principal for Beshenich Muir and Associates (BMA)

"Mark has been instrumental in helping us to develop the leadership development program for Global Leaders in Law, and we have been privileged to have him as one of our leadership speakers. In this book, Mark brings together many of the ideas, stories, and knowledge that he has shared with us over the last five years. He provides an excellent reference source for those who have attended his lectures as well as an introduction to some of his experiences of leadership throughout his career. I am sure Mark's new book will be a great success across the globe."

—Meena Heath
Founder and Global Ambassador, Global Leaders in Law

LEAD & INFLUENCE

LEAD & INFLUENCE

Get More Ownership, Commitment, and Achievement from Your Team

MARK FRITZ

WILEY

Cover design: Michael J. Freeland

Published by John Wiley & Sons, Inc., Hoboken, New Jersey.
Published simultaneously in Canada.

For general information about our other products and services, please contact our Customer Care Department within the United States at (800) 762-2974, outside the United States at (317) 572-3993 or fax (317) 572-4002.

Wiley publishes in a variety of print and electronic formats and by print-on-demand. Some material included with standard print versions of this book may not be included in e-books or in print-on-demand. If this book refers to media such as a CD or DVD that is not included in the version you purchased, you may download this material at http://booksupport.wiley.com. For more information about Wiley products, visit www.wiley.com.

ISBN: 978-1-118-73288-5 (cloth)

ISBN: 978-1-118-73289-2 (ebk)

ISBN: 978-1-118-73290-8 (ebk)

Printed in the United States of America

10 9 8 7 6 5 4 3 2 1

This book is dedicated to all the leaders who, over the years, have provided me with inspiration, insights, and ideas to take my own leadership and influencing skills to higher levels. I have learned something from everyone, and the more I have learned, the more I have noticed how important core leadership skills are when guiding others. These skills provide the foundation that enables leadership success.

CONTENTS

PART V AND FINALLY . . .   159

FOREWORD

In times of harsh business environments, like those in which we're living today, it's a tempting for business leaders to believe that *pressure creates energy* and that they should therefore be able to challenge what is condemned and eventually survive. But it's often in a downturn context that the staff's attitudes, feelings of inadequacy and lack of control, and misperception regarding what they can or cannot do—and the consequent sentiment of helplessness—primarily lead to performance deterioration. Sometimes, they can even prompt entire organizations or industries to go out of business.

The challenge for today's leaders is to find the middle point: where the energy created by the threat becomes the trigger for innovation or even for a turnaround. I believe that leaders' actions can help improve and sustain scopes of action for the staff, activities that promote creativeness and new ways of thinking. The difficult part is to foster this pedagogical attitude in the leaders.

And that's what makes *Lead & Influence* a must read. Mark Fritz's new book is a treasure for leaders who want to succeed by enhancing their coworkers' freedom to act and strengthening their attitude of ownership. Once again, Mark's prismatic gift of making complex concepts easy to understand enlightens us about the power of modeling the way and making the business vision *tangible and owned* by the organization's people. In *Lead & Influence*, Mark takes the reader through a journey of self-reflection, constantly reminding us that our leadership success is based on how well we and our people are learning with our experiences—and applying those lessons to our own lives.

This book provides leaders with insights on how our interactions with others can transform the understanding of the predominant logic of action, demands, and rules and help our coworkers improve and sustain scopes of action that promote creativeness and new ways of thinking.

—**Victor Vale**
Group HR Director of TAP-Portugal
Lisbon, 2013

PREFACE

Why Ownership Is Key to Your Leadership Success

When was the last time you washed a rental car? If you are like most other people, you probably never washed a rental car—and you probably know why. It's not *your* car, so it's not your responsibility to keep it looking clean. You don't have the same feeling of pride and ownership for the rental car as you would with your own car.

I have been working internationally for more than 30 years, and my work has required me to both lead and influence people across distances and cultures on a daily basis. It's also given me the chance to observe and learn from very successful leaders. Over these three decades, I noticed one key trait that allowed them to realize leadership success: all enabled a *feeling of ownership* regarding achievement in their people.

These leaders taught me that leaders succeed by getting people to *own* achievement, *not* by trying to control what people do. Truly great leaders know that their goal is to enable their people to create *their own* success, both individually and for their teams. The very best people and teams are doing it more for themselves than for their leaders. That's the power in the feeling of ownership.

What happens in your team when your people don't have the feeling of ownership for what they are being asked to achieve? Well, probably things such as people missing deadlines, a lack of teamwork to resolve problems quickly, or people simply not doing what they should be doing—clearly things you don't want to be happening. In these situations, your people simply rent their jobs versus owning them.

What do you do when your rental car has a problem? That's right, you take the car back. That's pretty much what your employees are doing if they are renting their jobs. Instead of being focused on finding a solution on their own—and thereby taking ownership for the solution—they simply come back to you for the easy answer to their problem. In other words, they're just parking the problem and putting it aside for someone else to solve.

In situations in which your people are renting their jobs, you begin to run your team on your own personal capacity, feeling as through *you* have to provide all the answers, instead of using your team's capacity. When your people own the achievement, you begin using the team's ability to drive performance.

Encouraging your people to take on the feeling of ownership is essential to the success of today's leaders, especially those who are required to lead people across distances and cultures.

Distances and cultures are the real acid tests for leadership. In fact, one of the best ways to see if your people have strong leadership skills is to give them someone to lead across distances or across cultures because of the nuances inherent in each:

- *Across distances:* At a distance, you cannot really see what your people are doing each day. You can't manage their activities closely and tell whether they're doing what you want them to be doing—or not. If they aren't, you experience a loss in productivity. At a distance, you have to lead your people and monitor their *achievement of outcomes* versus trying to manage their daily activities. If your people don't own what you are asking them to achieve, then you will have to constantly follow up to ensure that they're making progress. You then ultimately spend all your time checking in on their assignments and commitments, leaving little or no time for you to invest in your team's future.

- *Across cultures:* It's a little more difficult to tell people from other cultures specifically *what to do*, because things are accomplished differently in every culture. Each culture has its own influencing approaches and processes to get things done. You have to set clear outcomes for them to achieve, and again, monitor their progress and achievement. Trying to direct detailed activities across cultures often results in culture clashes. It's imperative that you define and communicate clear outcomes and reinforce your key principles or boundaries. This allows your multicultural employees to find solutions on their own, solutions that match the way they're accustomed to doing business.

Throughout the book will be some examples and guidance of how to lead across distances and cultures and how to get each individual and the team as a whole to take ownership for achievement.

It's also impossible to manage activities across distances and cultures and have any semblance of a personal life. Attempting to do so usually leaves you in a place where you've simply run out of day. You have to *lead* in such a way that encourages your people to *own* their achievements—and their results.

This book is not designed to be read once and then put up on the shelf. It is meant to be a reference for you when you need to remind yourself of those core leadership mind-sets and habits that can make the biggest difference to your leadership. As such, the key takeaways at the end of each chapter highlight important lessons. They also provide a chance for you to reflect and ask yourself about your own leadership.

The ultimate goal of this book is to help you to **extend your leadership impact** within your team—*without* extending your day.

Preface (Takeaways)

- Your leadership success exists in proportion to your staff's ownership for achievement.

- Differences in distances and cultures are the real acid tests for leadership and situations in which you must lead outcomes.

- Strong mind-sets and habits will extend your leadership without extending your day.

Your Key Reflection Questions

- To what level do your key people feel ownership for your team's achievement?

- What visible behaviors do they display that indicate to you that they feel ownership?

- What are the important elements of the culture that encourage your people to take ownership for your team's achievement?

ACKNOWLEDGMENTS

There are so many people I would like to acknowledge with respect to helping me bring this book to you.

First, my wife, who continues to be a fantastic partner and supporter of my passion for leadership.

Second, to great support from my publisher John Wiley & Sons, Inc., and in particular Christine Moore, who helped me make this book the best it could be.

And last, to all the leaders whom I had the pleasure to both listen to and interact with over the years; I continue to learn every day from all of you . . . as leadership is both a skill and an art that you never stop learning.

Core Leadership Skills

The leaders I have learned from over the years personified these skills. As such, I wanted to highlight two resources that I have continuously used to increase my inspiration, insights, and ideas on leadership.

1. *The Entrepreneurial Thought Leaders Lecture Series*

   I particularly want to dedicate this book to Tina Seelig and everyone connected with the Stanford Technology Ventures Program (STVP) Entrepreneurship Corner. I have been listening to the *Entrepreneurial Thought Leaders* lecture series podcasts for years and have found them to be a fantastic resource for leadership learnings. Thank you, ETL and all the leaders in your lecture series over the years.

Website: http://ecorner.stanford.edu/podcasts.html

2. *HBR IdeaCast Podcasts*

A big thank you goes out to the HBR IdeaCast, from the publishers of *Harvard Business Review*, Harvard Business Press, and hbr.org. These podcasts feature breakthrough ideas and commentary from the leading thinkers in business and leadership. Over the years, I have found the interviews with today's leading thinkers full of insights and ideas to help take my own leadership thinking further.

Website: http://blogs.hbr.org/ideacast/

Part I
Mind-set of Achievement and Collaboration

The mind-set you bring to your leadership role has a big impact on how you behave and provides the driving focus for your team. Team success comes more quickly and easily when leaders have a strong achievement and collaboration mind-set *and* have the ability to get their team to adopt it.

Success is a team sport. When everyone in the team collaborates and is collectively focused on reaching the same goal, magical levels of performance can be achieved. Success starts with having an outcomes focus on achievement and clearly defining what *success* is, for both yourself and your team.

Mind-set of Achievement and Collaboration Chapters

Chapter 1: Thinking and Discussing in Outcomes versus Activities

Chapter 2: The Ultimate Outcome Is Success (And the *Why* behind It)

Chapter 3: Creating the Environment for Effective Collaboration

1 Thinking and Discussing in Outcomes versus Activities

There's a great story I like to tell that highlights the power of encouraging your people to take an outcomes-over-activities mind-set to their work. Many years ago, General W. L. "Bill" Creech took over the Tactical Air Command (TAC) in the US Air Force, which, at that time, was a team of more than 100,000 people across the world. Their job was to repair and maintain the airplanes.

When General Creech took over, the team was organized by function and computer notifications directed workers to aircraft in need of repair and maintenance. Believing in the power of teamwork, he reorganized the entire staff into teams and assigned these newly formed small teams specific airplanes to maintain. The teams focused on keeping their planes flying and shared best practices with one another. The result was that *all* the teams' performance increased dramatically. After the team restructuring was completed, General Creech visited his teams throughout the world and asked his staff how they liked this new way of working. On one occasion, a team member replied with a question back to the general:

"When is the last time you washed a rental car?"

That may sound like a strange response, but it indicated that the teams were now taking real ownership for ensuring the planes were safely flying—they were owning the outcome, a stark difference from their attitude before the restructuring. Before the restructuring they were focused on their own individual activities and not on the outcome—the plane safely flying.

Before: The teams were *activity*-focused, focused on whatever their individual tasks were for that day.

Now: The teams are *outcome*-focused, asking the overarching question, is the plane flying?

Being outcomes-focused, versus activity-focused, makes a huge difference. When staff focus on the activities, their focus is on staying busy. There is no force driving them to do anything differently than they did the day before. But when staff are focused on *outcomes*, their focus is on achievement—and with an achievement focus, they are motivated to look for better ways to reach the achievement faster.

It's no surprise then that successful leaders think and communicate using the *language of achievement.* They bring an outcomes mindset to everything they do and focus on instilling that mind-set in their people, too.

Here are a couple of comparisons between the language of achievement versus the language of activity:

Language of Achievement	Language of Activity
Talk in . . .	*Talk in . . .*
Outputs	Inputs
Deliverables	Tasks
Decisions	Discussions
Milestones	To-do lists

A leader of a global virtual team noticed the power of the language of achievement with her team. She began every conversation she had with her team, both one on one and as a group, with the outcome that needed to be achieved and the date it was needed by. Then they discussed how they would tackle the activities and meet the milestones. They always finished the conversation by reconfirming the outcome and key dates. She found that by always bookending the conversation, starting and ending with what needed to be achieved—the outcome—she was constantly reinforcing the achievement in her team member's minds.

Ownership for Achievement (Outcomes)

The general's team member comment about rental cars indicated that the teams now took ownership for the outcome (the plane flying), and they helped their fellow team members fix the plane faster. After all, if the plane had five problems and only four have been fixed, it's still not flying! With a focus on the outcome, the team members pitched in to help one another efficiently fix problems as they arose. In fact, they painted their team names on the side of the airplanes, which signaled real ownership.

Outcomes **drive ownership, and ownership drives commitment**.

The general did two things that are absolutely crucial for a successful team, especially when you are leading across distances and cultures:

1. *He injected positive competition (peer pressure) into the group.* He made team performance visible to everyone and fueled competition among the teams by tracking which teams could repair the planes the fastest and with the best quality. He had a strong quality and performance focus and instilled that focus in everyone in the teams. The importance of this positive competition and peer pressure is discussed further in Chapter 11. But suffice it to say, every successful team has some element of competition within it.

2. *He had teams share best practices (continuous improvement).* The general drove the teams to share their best practices with the

other teams so that the good things people were doing could be replicated across the entire organization. This best practice sharing drove better overall quality, performance, and pride throughout.

The general knew the importance of posing and answering the question, *Would you rather your people own or rent their jobs?* You'll see a big difference in their behavior depending on which of these they choose. There's also big difference based on whether people own what they are *doing* or own what you ask them to *achieve*.

Would you rather your people own an activity or own an outcome? This is another crucial distinction. When your people own only the activities and you discuss only these with them, you are speaking in the language of busyness. When you can compel them to own, and therefore talk about, outcomes, everyone is speaking the language of achievement.

That doesn't mean activities are never discussed. But smart managers always frame these activities' discussions with what needs to be achieved—the outcomes that those activities create.

Outcomes Are Both Visible *Results* and Visible *Experiences*

Consider the example of the teams repairing airplanes; the obvious visible result is the successful flying of the planes. But the visible experience or experiences might be the way the team interacts with the pilot. This is important in two particular situations: the team wants to *get the right information* from the pilot to fix any problems with the plane, and the team *wants the pilot to be confident* that the plane is in top working order and that all problems have been fixed.

The same applies to *your* team. You have both visible results you are focusing on achieving and targets for the *experiences* you want others to have (to feel) in achieving those results. You have both internal experiences (team experiences) and external experiences (for example, those involving customers, vendors, and partners).

Think about the experiences in your own life, such as flying somewhere. The result for you is getting from point A to point B. Your experience, on the other hand, is determined by the effectiveness of the service and how the airline personnel treat you—the things that affect how you *feel* about that airline. An experience creates a strong impact, because it is the feeling that stays with you long after you have forgotten the details of the flight.

A customer services group has both visible results and experiences. It must successfully process all customer orders while also successfully resolving every customer problem. From the customers' perspective, their experiences—their interaction with the customer service representative and how it made them think about the representative and the company—is what they will remember. To be successful, it is key that customer service representatives focus on the experience as well as the result.

So ask yourself, and ask your team: *What are the most important experiences that we deliver?* Sometimes, the outcomes that drive the largest influence with others are the visible experiences, because the successful outcome is always engaging people's feelings. Sometimes, however, the most important things aren't visible.

A Clear Direction and Pace

Successful leaders are focused on *direction and pace*. They know clearly where they want to take the team (the direction or goals) and want to get there as fast as they can (the pace). These leaders create a sense of urgency that drives the pace their people's work. Direction and pace are the most important criteria they use to decide whether to say yes or no to new initiatives or projects.

Successful leaders ask themselves, "Is this taking us in the right direction at the right pace?" These two elements determine the leader's focus and therefore the team's focus as well.

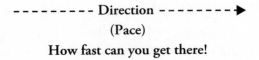

- - - - - - - - Direction - - - - - - - ➤
(Pace)
How fast can you get there!

When the direction is clear, the entire team feels the same sense of urgency; everyone takes more action and is clear on what they must do. In fact, *clarity* is probably the most important word in any language. Think about it: when you are not clear on something, it stops you from taking action. And if, as a leader, you are not clear on something, you will not communicate as clearly and effectively to your people.

There is a great saying: "If it is a mist in the pulpit, it is a fog in the pew."

In other words, if something isn't understandable in *your* mind, it will be even less so when you start speaking about it to others. Successful leaders create clarity in everything they do and say. You could even say that a leader's job is to bring clarity to their people, helping them to always see a way forward, and keep them moving in the direction of the teams' goals.

Define Outcomes to Achieve and Monitor Milestones

Successful leaders unambiguously define what needs to be achieved, or they *jointly* define this with their teams. They then ask their staff to report on the milestones throughout the journey toward this outcome.

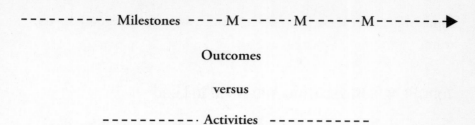

Will your people have more ownership for their milestones or yours? Obviously, theirs. Therefore, asking your people to discuss *their* milestones motivates them to take more ownership for the pace of progress toward the achievement, and this is extremely important when leading across distances and cultures. Because it's so difficult, almost impossible, in fact, to manage activities at a distance, you lead by following up on the achievement of *milestones* versus activities. And getting your employees to describe and feel enthusiasm for these milestones is what compels them to feel ownership for the pace of the achievement.

Of course, not all of your people will want to take ownership for outcomes. Some simply want to come to work and complete the activities they are told to do. Every organization has activity-focused people who aren't motivated and want someone else to do all their thinking for them. These are not the right people to have on your team; they lack that essential desire to own achievement.

However, they're not a lost cause entirely. Giving these people small outcomes to achieve and then gradually increasing those outcomes is one way to start motivating them—and testing to see whether they will ever start embracing that sense of ownership.

Small outcomes (o) to larger outcomes (O)

If, however, you find that some people never want to take ownership for the outcomes—small or large—you likely have to work on moving them out of the team. If you or other team members always have to do the thinking for these people, then they'll keep everyone else from achieving *their* own outcomes. It takes strength to do something about these people, but it's necessary for the good of your team.

Your People Reveal How You Need to Lead

There is another benefit in asking your people for their milestones: it helps you gauge your own leadership effectiveness. The quality of their answers will reveal to you how successful you have been in leading them and what you may need to change.

Team members who set milestones that make sense and link to other initiatives can be trusted to deliver without having to be closely monitored. Conversely, team members who provide milestones that don't connect to the team's initiatives likely require close monitoring to ensure they successfully deliver. This kind of assessment allows you to be a more effective leader, which helps you and your team deliver more—*and* saves you time.

What are the most important criteria for setting milestones? This is important, because the clarity and quality of the milestones drive both the achievement and the pace that the achievement is delivered. The right milestones:

- Mark a clear achievement that is visible within and outside the team.

- Are measurable (quantitatively or qualitatively) in some universally agreed-upon way.

- Timed to match up with other key initiatives where there are shared milestones.

Your real power of influence as a leader comes from your *questions*, not your answers. The more you ask, the more you understand your people—and the better you can determine how to lead them in ways that prompt their best performance. Remember, without asking questions, you're merely guessing, which is not a sound strategy for anything.

There are three key questions you can ask to uncover some important information to lead your team well:

1. **What's the plan?**

   What will you achieve, and what are the milestones to get there?

2. **Who's in charge?**

   Which individuals, team, or teams are responsible for delivering it?

3. **Compared with what?**

   How are you defining good performance? What are you comparing it against?

The last one was of particular interest to General Creech. He knew that "good" is only good by comparison.

So ask yourself, *What comparison am I using to understand whether my team is delivering good performance?* People take more ownership to improve their performance when it is clear what good is and why it's crucial to reach that level of performance. If they don't have a benchmark or a target, they miss the incentive to use their creativity to look for new and better ways to do their job and improve their performance.

One of the most important jobs leaders have is to set the right expectations for their team's performance, and that starts by making it clear what they are using to compare good and bad performance. Successful leaders are constantly seeking external benchmarks and best practices in order to give their employees a performance comparison that will both stretch them to higher levels of performance *and* demonstrate that it is something within their reach, making it *achievable*.

Ownership Enables Pride

The general's target went beyond outcomes, ownership, and commitment; it also included pride. He knew that people who take pride in what they do will do it well and continuously search for ways to do it *better*.

In the airplanes example mentioned earlier, team members were first focused on only their activities (fixing the engine, loading the weapons, etc.). That brought them some satisfaction if they did it well and were recognized for it. However, after they began working as a team, focusing on the outcome of the plane flying, they felt more pride in their own work because it went beyond just a single person's activity; it was a team effort. Successful teams have team members with both individual and team pride.

Your staff will take more pride in achieving an outcome than simply fulfilling a task. This is why it is so important to maintain a focus on outcomes. Your employees will be prouder of what they do when you *focus, monitor*, and *recognize* their achievements.

Unfortunately, pride can get a bad rap in today's world because it's often confused with ego. However, ego is different; it is *pride without humility*. Pride + humility = *magic*, and *that* is when you get the top performance from the people in your team. When you instill pride in your people and team, they will truly deliver magical performance for you.

What are the ways you can create pride in achievement for your team? In every team, what you talk about comes about. Successful leaders continually recognize and celebrate their people and teams' accomplishments. Pride, like trust, is not a given; it's something that you must constantly reinforce through recognition.

Recognition comes in many forms, but there are some key ingredients that create stronger pride:

- Provide timely recognition. Give it when the achievement was accomplished.

- Be specific, and highlight good behaviors that enabled that achievement.

- Recognize both individuals and teams. It takes both personal and team ownership.

- Link the achievement and recognition to the team's goals and vision.

- Be consistently different. Recognition in the same ways all the time becomes boring.

Drive Outcomes-Focused Meetings

Meetings are common in all organizations and industries. Chances are, if you were to ask your staff, they would say that they attend far too many meetings. In fact, they might be rushing off to the next (often unproductive) meeting and not even have time to answer.

How often do you hear someone say, "We need a meeting to discuss this"? There is probably a smile (or a scowl!) on your face right now, since you've likely heard that expression many, many times. Consider this as well: Is discussion an activity or an outcome? It's an activity—which is why meetings are often so ineffective.

When you're framing your meetings with an activity focus, all you get is more and more discussion. Successful meetings are focused on *outcomes*—and meetings can really have only three outcomes:

1. An agreed-upon decision
2. An agreed-upon action
3. Consistent understanding (meaning staff will take consistent action after the meeting)

What are you thinking when you leave a poorly run meeting? Probably something like, "What a waste of time *that* was." And that's not something your organization can afford. So many leaders create problems for themselves because they're not able to run good meetings. If you happen to be one of these visionary leaders who does not like the discipline and structure involved in organizing meetings, then get somebody close to you to run the meeting for you. You can't afford to have your people leaving your meetings thinking, "This was a waste of time."

This seven-step process will help you run more outcome-focused meetings:

1. *Successful outcome:* What's the outcome for everyone?
2. *Key topics to cover:* What needs to be discussed to achieve the outcome?
3. *Right participants:* Who needs to be there?
4. *Prework needed:* What work must be done before the meeting to achieve the outcome?
5. *Participants to talk to:* What individual alignment is necessary for faster meeting alignment?
6. *Agenda:* How can we structure the timing to achieve the outcome?
7. *Follow-up:* What do we need to do after the meeting to take follow-up action?

Do you ever need to lead conference calls with people in different locations around the world? If you do, you know how challenging it can be to keep everyone's attention on the call and away from e-mail. Experienced conference call leaders do one thing to keep their people's attention: they say the names of people in the different locations throughout the call. They know that when people hear their names, they stop checking their e-mail and doing other tasks and immediately return their attention to the call—often wondering what was said about them. These leaders find a way to refer to their people's input—and by saying people's names throughout the call, they command their attention the entire time.

The first question you should always ask when you're invited to a meeting is: "What's the successful outcome for this meeting?" It will force the meeting holder to articulate what he or she really wants to achieve, versus only what he or she wants to discuss—and it may cause the leader to realize that a meeting might *not* be necessary, after all.

When you speak in outcomes (the language of achievement), including during meetings, you get more ownership, commitment, and achievement from your team.

What Stops Leaders from Taking an Outcomes Focus?

It is all about what a leader needs to feel in control. People like certainty. They don't like drastic change that leaves them uncertain about what to focus on—what they need to do and how they need to do it. Leaders are the same; they want to feel that they're in control. Unfortunately, the higher you rise in a team, the more uncertainty you're faced with and the more ambiguous your job's focus will be. You don't have as many bosses above you, and you're expected to define your own work and motivate yourself to do it.

So what do you need to feel in control? This question drives a lot of our behaviors, especially as leaders. If you're the type of person who needs detailed information on the status of every project, your inbox will always be full and you'll be constantly inundated with questions from people who are relying on you for the answers. They will rely on your micromanaging to prevent them from making bad decisions. This way of working becomes impossible for leaders across distances and cultures, unless you want to give up more of your personal and family life to do it.

Leadership Behaviors Are Shaped by This Need for Control

Although a great number of leaders perceive access to information as a way of being in control, others know that they can gain the same level of control by looking at whom they put in charge of things. In other words, if the people they put in charge or allocate to their teams feel ownership of the outcomes (the achievements), they can take responsibility without the leader needing to micromanage their activities. They achieve a sense of control by putting trust in key people and monitoring the achievement of outcomes rather than managing and controlling activities.

Real control is through *people*, not information.

When your people own achievement, you have more control. There's a big difference between gaining control through monitoring achievement and milestones and doing so by managing activities and dealing with a constant stream of updates.

What Do Your Inbox and Calendar Say about You?

Other people can infer a great deal about your leadership style simply by looking your received and sent e-mails, as well as the appointments and meetings you have in your calendar. There are two key factors that drive them both: one is control, which we've already discussed; the other is choice.

Choice—Driver's Seat or Passenger's Seat?

Your leadership and your life are driven by your choices, and your most important choice is whether to take the driver's seat or the passenger's seat. With respect to e-mail, there are far too many people who let their inbox drive their day. It's always your choice as to what meetings you choose to attend or not. Successful leaders know that their greatest power is their power of choice, and they never surrender their power of choice to their people or others around them.

What It Takes to Feel in Control?

As discussed earlier, the knowledge you must have to feel in control propels many of your daily and weekly behaviors. It prompts the e-mails you send and the information you request, as well as your need for more meetings to stay updated on everything you feel you need to know. With so much information available to all of us these days, the key is deciding what specific information you need to take action. Said in another way: you can take more action and achieve success faster when you decide what you *don't* need to know.

First, let's take a look at what your inbox reveals about you:

- If you look to your inbox to decide what to do next, then others drive your day.

- If you ask to be informed about everything, then you will be informed about everything.

Second, let's look at what your calendar might reveal:

- If your days are booked solid with meetings, you're letting others drive your day.

- If you have 1-hour meetings, you tend to become discussion focused instead of outcome focused.

- If you don't block off your best times for you, you're surrendering to others' priorities.

What would your inbox and calendar say about your leadership style? Do they indicate that you're outcomes or activities focused? And what do they say about your need for control? It's a good exercise to review these and ask yourself those questions. The answers will indicate how you use your power of choice and what it takes for you to feel in control.

Thinking and Discussing in Outcomes versus Activities (Takeaways)

- Package all your conversations in the language of achievement; that is, speak in terms of outcomes.

- Ask your people for the milestones. Their responses reveal to you how they need to be led.

- Drive outcomes-focused meetings; you cannot afford to waste your people's time.

Your Key Reflection Questions

- Have I focused all my conversations and meetings on achievement and outcomes?

- What are the most important visible results and experiences that my team delivers?

- How would my people know, based on my behaviors, that I'm in charge of my inbox and calendar?

2 The Ultimate Outcome Is Success (And the *Why* behind It)

I've spoken to a fair number of executives over the years, but one conversation stands out in my mind. This particular individual talked about how he achieved all of what he wanted for his career but didn't really have any type of family life. When I asked about his professional goals, he told me, "I had crystal clear goals for the career I wanted." But when I asked whether he had goals for the journey or how he wanted to live his life, what do you think he said? You guessed right. He said, "I had no goals at all."

When you take an outcomes focus, the ultimate outcome is success. Therefore, the way you *define success* both for yourself and your team is key. Personally, it provides the target for you to use your potential; it also provides the target for your team to achieve the performance you want from them. The most successful leaders look at success as an *and*, not as an *or*.

Success Is an *And*

Success is both a destination and a journey—it's about achieving what you want and enjoying the trip while getting there.

-------Journey -------▶ Destination

However, some people think of success only in terms of the destination. These people tend to ignore and neglect their personal and family lives to achieve their career objectives. Others concentrate *solely* on the journey and spend a lifetime trying to figure out their destination. True success is really about both the journey and the destination.

Is success an and *or an* or *for you?* For the executive in the opening story, success was an *or*.

Successful and happy executives—and their teams—*always* view success as an *and*. It is both the results you want to achieve, and the behaviors that are going to enable those results. So how do you treat it?

- - - - - - - - - Behaviors - - - -▶ Results

Many leaders and members of the corporate world often want a job or an assignment for just 18 months. They want to create an annual plan, drive their people hard to deliver the great results defined in the plan, and then get promoted. With this approach, they don't have to worry about improving people's behaviors or the culture. You can push people for a year to deliver great results, but you cannot repeat it and drive consistent great results for three or more years unless you also expend efforts to improve the behaviors, culture, and processes.

The Why Powers Ownership for Success

When you have a powerful reason—a why—for what you want to achieve, you take more action. Your team and your people need a why, too!

The success equation is simple:

$$\textbf{Why} > \textbf{How}$$

In other words, the *why* will always be larger than the *how*.

Don't believe it? Think about how this equation relates to your own life. How many times have you wanted to do something but the how was difficult and your why just wasn't strong enough to drive you to take action. You didn't take action, did you? But I bet you can think back to those times when your why was so strong that you would do anything (take any action) to achieve it.

Look at the person who wants to quit smoking. He wants to quit, but the why and the how are having a battle with each other. The person may quit and start again, quit and start again, never quite being able to make the change permanent. Then, he goes to the doctor, and the doctor says, "You have a spot on your lung." Suddenly, the person quits just like that. In other words, the why ("If I don't stop, I could die") just dramatically became greater than how (the difficulty of quitting).

If you ask one of your team members to do something difficult but she doesn't know why, she will likely put off getting started on it. She may even wait until the last possible moment to work on it or wait until you remind her to do it.

There are three keys for creating the why: clarity, passion, and visibility. When leaders create a *clear* direction/goal and their people are *passionate* about it, this creates the energy to do whatever it takes to achieve it. However, there are times when passion is not enough; in these cases, leaders need to create the energy in their people to do it anyway. That's where visibility of what is being asked to achieve is important. When others in the team know they need to achieve it, then they focus themselves to do it, because they don't want to look bad in front of their peers by not delivering. This peer pressure and how to create it is discussed in Chapter 11.

Your team also suffers when this equation is out of balance, when why < how. When your people find the how difficult and don't really have a why or understand it, they simply avoid doing whatever *it* is. And you're not there to see them not doing it if you're leading people across distances and cultures. You cannot be there all the time to push them to do it.

Which drives you to take more action: getting it emotionally or intellectually?

If you're like most people, *emotion* drives more action. The why >
how equation does not take an intellectual or logical view but rather
an emotional one. When your people stop taking action, they likely
feel that the difficultly of the *how* outweighs the *why*.

One of the most important jobs of leaders is to define and communicate the why for their teams. You know the acronym CEO, chief
executive officer; the *executive* could easily be replaced with *explaining*.

CEO = chief explaining officer

CEOs have a strong leadership team that can create the what and
the how, but the why is the motivating force that drives the direction
and the pace that powers the organization's success.

The real power of why comes when you align your team's why
with your key people's personal whys; your key people want the
chance to showcase their talents to others. This is the perfect time to
give them opportunities to lead projects that provide them visibility
beyond your team and ideally even outside the company, both with
vendors and customers. The more visibility you give your key people,
the more motivated they will be.

Team why ◄ - - - - - - Aligned - - - - - - - ► Personal why

Everyone thinks of money as the key motivator. But money
doesn't really motivate; it focuses people. Therefore, the why becomes
important to provide something beyond a focus: the motivation.

Having a very clear focus and a powerful why behind it will
engage your entire mind to help you both see and take more action.
Consider the following example on the power of the subconscious
mind and having a very clear focus.

Think about when you bought your last car. You studied the bro-
chure, took a test drive, and fell in love with the idea (the picture) of

you owning that car. You were building *why* you needed to buy that car. By the time you bought that car, the why was so big that you would have felt terrible if you *didn't* buy it! You probably started to notice, as you were driving around at that time, many more cars just like the one you just bought. There were just as many on the road a few months before, but you never noticed them. Why? Because you built the why so strong on needing that car that your subconscious mind was pointing them out to you everywhere you drove. You didn't get up in the morning and decide to go look for that type of car all day long, did you? Your subconscious mind pointed them out without you even thinking of it.

The same thing happens when you have such a strong belief in something: it becomes a powerful focus for your subconscious mind to act upon. As you go through your day, your subconscious is pointing out people you meet who can help you reach what you want. If you believe strongly enough, your subconscious mind will help you see it and achieve it. You can imagine the power behind building the belief to achieve what you want. The more time you invest in building this belief and getting what you want, the more opportunities you will see to achieve it.

Successful leaders understand this power of the subconscious; that's why you see them constantly reinforcing the focus for their team in all different ways. It can be through regular updates or those subtle questions leaders ask their people throughout the day. These leaders know that the more their people maintain a strong focus, the more the entire mind (both the conscious and subconscious) will help them see opportunities and drive them to action to deliver the results within that focus.

The subconscious controls more of your daily behaviors than you think. Need proof? *Tell me your next thought.* You can't . . . because it's your subconscious mind that is triggering your next thought. You enlist your subconscious mind in helping you by constantly giving it a very clear focus on the outcome(s) you want and then repeating the focus in your mind. Your subconscious uses that focus to trigger more thoughts and ideas to achieve it.

When you give your people a strong focus, and both explain and personalize the why for them, they begin to see more chances to take action. And all of a sudden, just like the car in the previous example, the opportunities are everywhere.

Pull and Push Power

Successful leaders use a combination of pull and push: they communicate a powerful why that pulls people toward wanting to do what they need to. The push power comes from the leader and generally makes people feel as though they *have* to do something.

But push can be overused. When that happens, leaders will lose a portion of their powers with each successive use. Successful leaders know this and use a combination of both pull (the why) and push (their position) to drive their people to achieve the outcomes and deliver their performance commitments.

Why Power - - - - - -▶ **Pull your people to perform** - - - - -▶

Goes up with use

Position Power - - -▶ **Push your people to perform** - - -▶

Goes down with use

This concept of pull and push is especially crucial when leading across distances and cultures. Let's look at an example. Marybeth, a customer service leader in a multinational company, was promoted and took over two more teams in addition to her original team. She was used to leading people only in her own location and was suddenly leading employees in two more locations. She would tell them only what needed to be done, thereby essentially using only push.

Marybeth knew instinctively when she began managing these new teams that she couldn't push all three in the same way. However, she also thought she didn't have the time to invest in explaining the why. So, she simply tried to use the same approach she had with original team—and she was burning out very quickly as a result.

Marybeth's boss coached her about the need to explain the why and to make better use of her key people to help lead and manage her teams in the other countries. (You will read more about the importance of empowering your key people in Chapter 7.) It took three to six months before Marybeth was able to fully engage her key people, but it made a huge impact on her leadership. With her boss's support, she was able to explain the why and use more of a pull approach with her most critical employees. She began to trust her key people and let them make more of their own decisions about details (the activities). This freed her of managing all the activities and gave her time to contemplate and plan all three teams' future—to be a leader.

Ask yourself: *How was my use of pull and push this past week?* Use too much push, and your influence with your people plummets. Without sufficient pull, leaders are left feeling as though they must invest a great deal of their time to managing day-to-day achievement.

Doing What's Necessary

Most effective leaders will tell you that the key to their success comes down to doing what is necessary . . . *when* it is necessary.

Which are more successful: the leaders focused on enjoyable activities or enjoyable results? You would be amazed at the variety of the answers people give to this question. And it's actually a trick question; the correct answer is both. You need to enjoy 80 to 90 percent of what you do, or you will never realize world-class experiences or results. However, your clients and customers don't pay you to enjoy yourself; they pay you for enjoyable results. Therefore, you need both.

For most leaders, there is something in the middle that creates most of your headaches: the nonenjoyable activities, or what you may call necessary evils.

Enjoyable activities – – – Nonenjoyable activities – – – ▶ Enjoyable results
(Necessary evils)

Do you have to motivate your people to do what they enjoy? Not really. You have to motivate them to do what they *don't* enjoy: the necessary evils.

These necessary evils can range from uncomfortable conversations to data collection to reports that require especially detailed and difficult thinking to get clear on the right approach.

Those who lead at a distance can't see when employees are routinely avoiding the nonenjoyable activities. And for every day they procrastinate working on them, there's a loss in productivity. This is why making it clear what needs to be achieved—and why it needs to be achieved—is so crucial: it will help people power through tasks they don't enjoy, because they want to get to the achievement (the results) on the other side. The more visible you can make your desired outcomes, the more tangible—and accessible—they'll feel to your employees. You want them to feel the need to do those necessary evils *without being told to.*

Successful leaders tend to tackle do the nonenjoyable tasks at the beginning of the day. They know how important it is not to avoid these activities—because if your people see you avoiding them, it sort of gives them permission to avoid them, too. As a leader, you are in show business, and your personal ownership is visible to your people every day.

Many leaders turn doing these necessary evils into a game. One person I know gives himself a time limit to complete them by and then plays special productivity music in the background to create the right environment to just do it. Another writes down the necessary evils on sticky notes and puts them on her desk. The desk looks messy with all those notes on it, and that drives her to complete the necessary evils before receiving her first visitor.

What's your best method for tackling your necessary evils? Remember, your day can only gets better when you get these out of the way as early as possible.

Don't Wait for the Inspiration

Every successful leader shares a habit in regard to necessary evils to how they treat those nonenjoyable activities. They don't wait for *inspiration* to take action on them; they focus on creating a habit to do them without needing the inspiration. These leaders know that:

Action precedes inspiration.

It is not the other way around; inspiration isn't required to take action. You must invest the time to make a habit of doing the necessary. Smart leaders don't make too many changes at once; they focus on only one or two key habit changes at a time.

If you're waiting for the inspiration to take action, you might want to turn that around and focus on creating the habit for action. Once successful leaders take action, their own internal drive and inspiration kicks in to keep going until they reach the outcome. Success in business and in life is about taking the first action.

Conditions That Create the Success

A successful entrepreneur once remarked about success in a way that might seem strange at first. He said, "Entrepreneurs do not set out to create success. They set out to *create the conditions* that create the success."

If you think about this, you see how true this statement is. If you are an entrepreneur who is focused only on your company's success and you need to be there all the time to keep the success going, then when do you have time to start your next company? You don't. This concept is as crucial for leaders as it is for entrepreneurs. If you cannot find a way for your team to perform without you always being there, then you are going to have to always be there—which means you can't be anywhere else.

This is, of course, never the case for entrepreneurs who have started several successful companies. It is impossible for them to personally lead the day-to-day outcomes that are necessary for all their companies' successes. They have learned to develop the conditions that create the success.

What conditions have you established that enable your people to create success? This could be your highest leveraged focus—the more you put these conditions in place, the more your team creates the success without you having to be there all the time. For most leaders, it involves:

1. Having the *right people* in the right places.
2. Establishing the *right culture* that reinforces the right behavior and performance.
3. Providing the *right offering* that customers love and that challenges the people to be their best.

It's crucial to invest some time *today* to think about the conditions that enable your people to create the success for your team, because this could become your highest leveraged focus. The more you focus on establishing these conditions, the more time you have to focus on the strategy and direction for your team, as well as for a personal and family life.

When you invest time to define success for your team and the conditions that enable them to create that success, your focus as the leader of the team becomes much clearer:

1. To continuously communicate to the team what success looks like and why

2. To enable the conditions so that your team can go create it

The Importance of the Culture

Success comprises the results you want for your team and the behaviors that will deliver it, both today and in the future. A team culture is really just a set of group behaviors, the sum of your team member's behaviors. If people share more of the key behaviors needed for the team to collaborate and create the success, then the more success your team with have.

How would you describe the culture you need for your team's success? What shared behaviors will help your team deliver success now and deliver even greater success in the future? These are important questions to consider when building a strong team that can deliver beyond today. There is ongoing debate about the difference between leaders and managers; I don't want to get into that here. However, there is one focus that is consistent with every successful leader I have interacted with or observed: they all had a strong focus on building and reinforcing the right culture for their teams. In other words, they treated success as an *and*, and they knew culture was important for the team to deliver consistent results.

What are you doing to both build and reinforce your team's culture each week? I often ask this question in my mentoring or discussions with leaders, and there is one thing I have noticed. Successful leaders can respond instantly, because they have focus on the culture they need to build and reinforce and are taking actions on a weekly basis to make that culture a reality. Other leaders, however, have to stop and think a few minutes in order to respond.

- - - - - - - Behaviors (Culture) - - - ▶ Results

Remember, success is an *and:* it's about not only delivering the team's results but also developing the people in the team and the culture of the team to deliver even better results every year. Good leaders deliver results. Great leaders deliver results and cultivate a culture that will deliver results even after they leave the role.

The Ultimate Outcome Is Success (And the Why *behind It) (Takeaways)*

- The equation of success is why > how; that is: Every leader is a chief explaining officer.
- Focus on creating the conditions that enable your people to achieve success.
- Successful leaders know that action precedes inspiration, so they complete the necessary evils early in their day.

You Key Reflection Questions

- How did I use pull and push this past week to get things achieved?
- What are the conditions that enable my people to create success when I'm not around?
- What am I doing to create and reinforce the right culture for my team?

3 Creating the Environment for Effective Collaboration

Many leaders have an "I know it when I see it" attitude toward collaboration. However, successful leaders are always focused on encouraging behaviors that enable collaboration to take place—*without* them always needing to facilitate it. To say it another way, they are focused on advancing habits that compel collaboration in their own staff. One international executive judged whether the right collaboration was happening by observing whether his people were picking up the phone and calling one another. He figured that if people phoned one another to discuss an issue, then they must know and trust one another enough to have the conversation. Otherwise, they would simply send e-mails and copy the world to cover their a**es.

To successfully lead across distances and cultures, you need people who collaborate well. They cannot constantly be coming to you to facilitate the discussion *among* the team members.

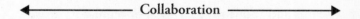

Collaboration

Success means getting your people to communicate across the team *without* always coming to you—that's real collaboration. When people are collaborating, you have the foundation to get genuine team ownership.

Collaboration is enabled by three main things, in this order:

1. Trust
2. Information sharing
3. Processes

However, because collaboration is essentially linked to people and the environment and culture within which they work, collaboration is never a constant. In fact, driving successful collaboration is like trying to solve a version of the Rubik's Cube where the squares keep changing colors. Successful leaders know that developing people who trust and share information with one another provides the flexibility to adapt to changing conditions, in both people *and* the environment.

Can your team be successful if people follow only documented processes? If you're like many other teams, you're probably answering no. If this is true, then trust and information sharing are driving the success of your team, and those are your informal processes. You can quickly identify an immature or an ineffective leader by asking, "What is your *first priority* in fixing the problem?" If it's simply to create a new process, then you know you've got a leadership problem!

If your people don't trust one another and don't share information, they will create a complex process. A leader's key priority, then, is to drive trust and information sharing throughout the team. People who have this kind of rapport require fewer processes to get things accomplished (and will create far simpler processes, too).

A few teams and industries, for legal or regulatory reasons, may need more formal processes in place. However, these teams will never achieve innovation on those processes until trust and sharing are constant.

These three collaboration priorities—trust, information sharing, and common processes—provide something you could call glue. It's what holds the team together, and it provides the foundation for effective teamwork and performance.

How is the glue in your team? There's a great outcome that helps you identify whether you have the right glue for your team, especially if team members are working in different locations and form different cultures: the previously mentioned phone test. *Are your people willing to pick up the phone if they have a problem or an opportunity?* If so, then that means they are dealing with things in real time, not just sending along another e-mail. When your people deal with problems or opportunities in real time (right away), you have strong glue and a more productive team.

Trust

Trust is the key enabler when leading across distances and cultures. When you cannot see what others are doing, you can't tell them exactly what to do differently (because, as we know, things get done differently in other cultures). You have to be able to trust your team members. One of an international leader's top priorities is to create and maintain team-wide trust, especially with key people.

One way to gauge the level of trust in your culture is to see how team members communicate bad news. If you have high trust, bad news seems to travel almost as fast as good news, which is key for you as a leader. You cannot do anything about bad news unless you know about it, and the sooner you're aware, the more options you have in how to deal with it. In fact, the way you handle bad news as a leader has a huge impact on your team's culture. Come down hard on the bearer of bad news, and you will never again hear about bad news when you should.

If you find the trust level is not where you need it to be, you can increase it through frequent communication and discovery of shared interests. People trust people they know and speak to often. Consider your own experiences: you likely have more trust issues with people you don't routinely communicate with or with people you communicate with about only specific work issues. Increasing communication facilitates increased trust, which further reinforces better communication and collaboration.

Shared Common Interests

As mentioned in the previous section, one thing that builds an especially strong foundation for trust, especially across distances and cultures, is for your people to learn more about what other employees do outside of work. The following is a story that illustrates this in a great way.

A very successful actress was interviewed on TV and asked how she played a part that was totally different from who she was—a different personality, different mind-set, and so forth. She answered: "I focus on the thing that is in common between me and the person I am playing, however small it is, and I *focus only on that* first. Then, I gradually work my way into the part."

The same is true for developing trust between team members. When you find the common interest between you and others, you always have a way to start your conversations.

| —— Interests —— | *Shared* | —— Interests —— |

This is especially crucial when your people are located in different cities or even countries and don't share the same physical space. If you can find that common link, you won't hesitate to address issues in real time.

Let's say that you know another person in a work capacity only. If you have an issue, you are less likely to pick up the phone to address it with the person directly; instead, will you'll probably resort to e-mail (maybe even cc'ing others). E-mail only delays conversations and results in a loss of productivity.

Do you know the common interest you have with your people, especially your key people? They can run the gamut from sharing the same hobbies; having children the same ages; coming from similar family backgrounds; liking the same sports teams, food, beer; and so on. There is *something* you can share with others, and when people find their common interests, conversation ensues and always leads to learning more about each other. The more your people know about one another, the closer they become—and the more trust they develop.

A European project leader was asked to consolidate customer service operations across various countries and sites into a single location. He was charged with implementing the core best practices in all sites around the world before the consolidation. If this weren't done, it would be a nightmare to manage the multiple sites and impossible to get the operational savings and financial benefits sought.

The way forward was to get customer service representatives from each site to share and implement their best practices. However, cost constraints prevented them from traveling and meeting face to face to work on this, so they had to move the effort forward by working together virtually.

To help get them started, the leader asked all the customer service representatives to create a presentation on themselves: both what they do at work and what they do at home. Each slide in the presentation had to contain a picture of something from work or home. Each person had time to introduce himself or herself in an effort to uncover common interests among the staff. These ice-breaker sessions resulted in building a strong personal link across the customer services representatives, which the leader credited for the successful adoption of the best practices they developed.

Common interests are the foundation of trust. When people get to know each other as *people*, not just colleagues, they are comfortable starting conversations on any topic.

High-Trust Teams

Trust problems must be addressed promptly. A lack of trust will create other problems in all other aspects of the team.

Consider these two teams: Team 1 is always happy, no one really argues, and all the meetings are happy ones. Team 2 argues about issues often, occasionally even crossing the line and making their comments a little too personal. Which team do you think is the higher-performing team? This might come as a surprise, but more often than not, it's the one arguing about the issues. Why? Because team members who don't even bother to disagree probably aren't really sharing what's on their minds. They don't trust each other enough to say what they're really thinking. Does this sound familiar?

Of course, it's also possible you have high trust but still little disagreement. In that case, you might have the wrong people on the team. There's an old saying that "if everyone is thinking alike, then someone might not be necessary." If you have a very strong team, then its members likely have different strengths, have different personalities, and think *differently*. People who offer a variety of perspectives and who trust one another are going to argue at *some* point—guaranteed.

Let's look at an example: An information technology (IT) team executive in a multinational company gathered his international project leaders together for a two-day meeting. There weren't enough resources to deliver all the projects, and the leaders were fighting over the limited resources. At times, the conversations were heated and occasionally became personal. During the first day, the executive's operations manager whispered into his ear, "Are you going to stop this?"

The executive replied, "No, it's important for people to express what they are thinking and feeling now versus when they are back in their countries."

Later that evening, the leaders went go-karting and then out for pizza and beer. After such a challenging day full of conflict, they needed this time to burn off the stress. In fact, the leaders who had been most vocal during the conversations earlier in the day confessed as much to the executive.

They needed to have those conversations, *and* they needed that go-karting/pizza and beer afterward to bring some perspective back. The leaders went into the second day of conversations with the same resources issue, but this time they talked far more constructively about how they could deal with it. Very often, there is greater teamwork and performance on the other side of conflict.

The Other Side of Conflict

Many leaders don't like to see conflict in their team, because they don't think they are strong enough to handle it. However, conflict is good for a number of reasons. For one thing, it means there is energy in the room; if your people are not passionately disagreeing, then they probably don't care too much about what they are doing. Second, conflict indicates diversity—it's reflective of having team members who see things from a range of viewpoints. That's great, because different thinking often brings stronger solutions—ones that hold up to the critical eyes from each direction. When leaders encourage their people to express their thinking and let the conflict out, they often get more valuable teamwork, solutions, and performance on the other side of that expressed conflict.

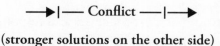

(stronger solutions on the other side)

Successful leaders are always looking out for potential team conflict—and they're always focused on doing something about it if they uncover it. If it's related to a business issue, they bring the conflict into a formal meeting setting to address it as a group. If the conflict is more personal, they bring the two parties together and talk through it. The only way to make real progress in *any* kind of conflict is to get people talking. All leaders know that unresolved conflict only intensifies and becomes more difficult to address. Addressing conflict in formal meetings prevents the issue from becoming a personal one and the subject of everyone's hallway or chat discussions.

Be strong enough to let your team members express their con-flict—stronger team solutions and performance are on the other side.

Information Sharing

For everyone to feel involved at the same level, every team member needs the same information. It is the only way to ensure that people have what they need to do their jobs effectively. This information must be accessible to teams from anywhere. Furthermore, teams must be able to access the information they need independently, without having to go through someone else to get it. This typically means the information needs to be self-service: accessible from some type of online database or website.

By ensuring that people have a readily accessible means of shar-ing information electronically, you free up your people to spend their time speaking with one another about more value-added topics. The increased productivity makes the investment in information architec-ture and systems well worth it.

Processes

Every successful team has clear processes and responsibilities. But given the pace at which business change is occurring, it's not enough to merely have good processes; you also need the ability to adapt and change those processes as business conditions change.

Both creating and modifying processes take time, and most teams make their processes so complex that the best people in the team run away when process work is asked for. So what's the answer?

You have to get the best people *in the room* or on the call!

Your best people will keep your processes simple, and they will find the most creative and efficient solutions. A good rule of thumb is to keep processes to a single page. If need be, you can make more detailed checklists to cover the options and details required to successfully service your customers. In every organization, the most important processes reinforce the expectations of the performance between departments and areas of the business.

Another good rule is to get the people who do the work to create the processes that will make it successful. Far too often people try to explain everything in the processes, and by trying to explain everything, it becomes too complex. By restricting your people to the length of the process documentation, you force them to be clear on the most important steps required to ensure the process works effectively. The processes provide the right boundaries for your team members to use their own business judgment in each of the different situations within the processes.

What type of processes are needed most? Especially in teams crossing distances and cultures, there has to be some structure in defining shared expectations in how work gets done. Information and completed work have to be shared across the team, and simple processes and templates make it easier for your people to do this without wasting time. Processes help reinforce the shared expectations your team members have. As in everything in business, the important thing is to keep these processes as simple as possible and not allow the processes to become bureaucratic.

Remember, you will need to champion the creation of the right common processes needed for your team. Working on processes is often not something that your people will find particularly motivating. This is where your leadership is needed most—to both communicate why (the pull) these processes need to be common and to have the right resources and timeline visible to push your people to do it.

Common Is Not a Reason!

When people are leading across distances and cultures, they often reach the conclusion that they should have a common approach across the team. The assumption is that people who follow the same processes and procedures will put forth the same output. However, it's crucial to remember what we learned from the beginning: different cultures do business differently. It therefore becomes less of a matter of driving commonality by implementing common processes and more a matter of aiming for consistent achievement and aligned outcomes.

Common in and of itself is not really a reason to do something. And remember: whatever you document, you must maintain.

Common Core Values

Having common core values usually means that people understand each other better, build trust faster, and perform more consistently. They no longer have to mold themselves to common processes for the sake of that commonality. Instead, they can focus on shared values and expectations—the drivers of real collaboration and consistency.

Common values provide a strong cultural foundation, and the number one value that helps you lead across distances, cultures, and any type of complexity is trust. The more people trust their teammates and the more trust exists as a core value, the more they are willing to say what they really think and the more they are open to sharing ideas with others. The more you drive trust between each member of your team, the more successful your team will be. This is at the core of very successful teams. They get their people to trust one another, which means sharing information rather than viewing it as a source of individual power. *Information becomes team power.* People want to share information and power instead of holding on to it, because these core values are known and shared. Successful leaders drive common values before common processes.

Collaboration Study Group

So how do you strengthen the glue of collaboration in your team? Involve your people in defining what's needed. Form a collaboration study group that's responsible for making recommendations regarding how to work together more effectively. This type of group is essential for international teams that work across distances and cultures. This is not just a one-and-done type of study; the people and business conditions are constantly changing, and new requirements often require new ways of working together to keep delivering on customer expectations in a productive way.

For example, the IT team of a multinational company went from country operations to virtual teams. People were now working daily with team members from other countries and reporting to leaders who were not in their home countries. To say the changes in the ways of working were significant would be an understatement. The team leader formed a virtual teams study group to assess how everyone could work together best and tasked them with recommending any new policies or procedures that could enable people to work together more effectively.

The group came up with recommendations on communications, meetings, and information sharing practices. In fact, they came back with one more thing the leader didn't ask for but appreciated: a list of leadership behaviors they wanted all the leaders of the team to have. There was nothing especially demanding on the list; most of the behaviors concerned the people development and recognition processes. The leader adopted the group's suggestions, which made a huge difference in team performance.

Will your people follow ways of working that they developed or ones that you as their leader have given them? Most likely, they prefer to follow parameters they've envisioned. So when possible, have your people make recommendations regarding how the team should be working. By doing so, they are defining the expectations they have for their fellow team members' behavior. You will read more about the importance of principles in Chapter 10.

The Mind-set of Options versus Answers

The level of collaboration in your team can make a big difference in the speed at which work gets done. When you have a team working across distances and cultures, your people's mind-sets can also play a significant role in how effective this collaboration becomes. People tend to have one of two mind-sets: answers or options.

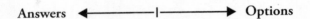

Answers ◄———————|———————► Options

1. *Answers mind-set:* These people are always searching for the perfect answer—and if you are working across distances and cultures, there are fewer perfect answers. When they can't find a perfect answer, they will freeze and stop taking action or come back to you, their leader, to provide the answer. They aren't as open to other opinions and often search for their perfect answers only within their own experiences.

2. *Options mind-set:* These people know that there are no perfect answers, only options. They know that their leader is paying them to imagine possible options and decide upon the best one for moving forward and taking action. They are flexible in the possible options and are open to input from everyone in order to reach a conclusion on the best option to progress.

Chances are, you'd prefer the majority of your people to have an options mind-set. This means that they're able to move forward and make decisions on their own. Those who take the answer mind-set will always need more support, because it is difficult for them to find the perfect answer in today's complex business environment.

Creating the Environment for Effective Collaboration (Takeaways)

- Everything starts with trust. It is never a constant, and it needs a focus every day.

- Encourage your people to pick up the phone if they have a problem or opportunity rather than exchanging e-mails.

- Help your people find their shared common interests; this is where their conversation starters are.

Your Key Reflection Questions

- How is our glue (our collaboration)? Our trust? Our information sharing? Our processes? Do we need to take some action to improve it?

- Are my people picking up the phone to call each other if they have a problem or an opportunity? Are they dealing with issues in real time?

- What am I and my team doing to increase the level of trust among team members?

Part II

Leading Yourself (Personal Ownership)

Leadership starts with being the right role model for your people, and that means *leading yourself well* before you can lead others. Chapters 4 through 6 are focused on the key aspects of leading yourself and how being the right role model drives more ownership for achievement within your team.

It is about understanding yourself, bringing the best you every day, and also understanding what *keeps you* in being the best you. The more you understand and lead yourself, the more you have the ability to adapt and successfully handle any leadership situations that come your way and be the best role model you can for your people. It begins with *you*.

Leading Yourself (Personal Ownership) Chapters

Chapter 4: Everything Starts with You Understanding You

Chapter 5: Strengthening Your Character and Focus (Your Foundation)

Chapter 6: Keeping Your Perspective and Balancing Your Stress

4 Everything Starts with You Understanding You

One executive was coaching a member of his leadership group who was struggling to influence a particularly important team member. No matter what he tried, he wasn't able to build a rapport with this person, and it was having a negative impact on the entire group's performance. The executive asked his leader an interesting question: "How much time do you invest in better *understanding yourself?*"

The leader was surprised by the question and didn't know what his boss was getting at. The executive noticed this and explained: "Early in my career, I was totally focused on increasing what I knew . . . about the business, the market, the customers, etc. As I climbed through the organization, I found that the foundation of my ability to influence others didn't come from what I knew about those things but from what I knew about myself. I realized that I couldn't build rapport with others unless I knew how I need to adapt my approach to gain that rapport—and that starts with knowing me."

Your own effectiveness and influence with others starts with *you understanding you.* The better you understand yourself, the better able you'll be to adapt your behavior and approaches to others, thereby increasing your influence with them.

◀ - - - - - - - - You - - - - - - | - - - - - Adapt - - - - - - ▶
(Influence)

Our emotions drive many of our behaviors, and it's crucial for today's international leaders to have high emotional intelligence. When you understand your emotions or what presses your hot buttons, you are better able to control those emotions when they have the potential to get the better of you.

Do you ever let your emotions drive you to overreact? The biggest problems ensue when leaders overreact to small things and underreact to big things. A yo-yo approach like this leads to people thinking that you're crazy, stressed, unfocused, and probably a few other things, too. These types of leaders compel employees to go to their boss's assistant and constantly ask, "How is the boss today? Is he (or she) in a good mood?" Your staff will also be reluctant to bring your bad news and often will then sit on that bad news for a quite a long time. And as people say, bad news does not age well.

Distance Magnifies Behavior

Conventional wisdom says that the more distance there is between others and you, the less impact you have on them. Although that can be the case in some ways, it is exactly the opposite for leaders with distances and cultures in the most important ways.

As a leader, you are in show business. Your people notice everything you do—and I mean everything. The saying that actions speak louder than words truly applies to leaders who lead across distances and cultures. You are on stage all the time. Your people tell stories about what you do and how you behave the same way they discuss what they hear about famous movie stars. In fact, the things they say about you travel faster and further than any formal communications *you* could ever create. Stories have a magnifying impact that grows stronger as they're repeated (and as those stories travel great distances).

Your communications become even more important and are replayed over and over again. When you are leading across distances, you often have fewer communications with your people, thereby making those communications that you *do* have even more critical.

Your staff's antennae will be up during those discussions, and they'll pay even more attention to what you say and how you behave. They are magnifying the success or lack of success of those communications and interactions.

For example, let's say you got upset during communication with Laura, one of your key people, and then didn't speak to her for a couple of weeks. Think about the effect that would have on her. She would naturally have that last interaction in mind and maybe even replay it and magnify until the next opportunity to communicate with you came along. In this way, distance—or infrequent contact—prompts those you lead to attach great importance to your behavior.

If you worked at the same location as Laura, ran into her at the coffee machine soon after that interaction, and shared a joke together, then that bad behavior wouldn't carry such significance for her. She might even forget it altogether. That contact you shared soon after the negative exchange would stop Laura from magnifying your prior tense exchange. But without that shared joke, the tense exchange is all she would have—and she would continue to magnify it.

People always fill a void—and often do so with a misunderstanding. If you are not communicating frequently with your people, then they are forming and magnifying their own perceptions of the situation. Lack of communication always prompts people to focus on their own perceptions, because they don't have any others to consider.

How frequent is your contact with your key people? Your behavior and frequency of contact plays a big role in what your employees consider important. The more they magnify the right thoughts, the more successful you are as a leader. If you can keep your people magnifying the right things, concentrating on the right thoughts, and telling the right stories about you, you'll be in good shape. You can achieve this by bringing the best you to your leadership role each and every day and making more frequent contact, even short, 5-minute calls, with your team.

How to Understand You

Leaders who understand themselves well didn't get there by accident. They thought about what would enable them to do so and developed the habits necessary to get a more complete picture of themselves, largely by focusing on feedback and reflection.

Feedback

Successful leaders are always asking others how they can improve their performance. Continuous feedback is one of the best ways to learn what you are doing well and what you could be doing better. Some leaders who aren't strong enough to take negative feedback or criticism often try to avoid it. However, if your ambition is to be in a higher role, you need to be comfortable with the criticism, because the higher the role, the more criticism there is.

One way leaders may be able to improve their willingness to hear feedback is to complete one of the many emotional intelligence assessments available nowadays. They help leaders understand how they handle their emotions, a key dimension in feedback responsiveness. One executive expressed his own experiences on investing in understanding himself in this way: "The more I was willing to hear feedback (or criticism) and to actively seek it out, the more I began to understand about myself and the faster I began to grow."

Reflection

Based on both their own experiences and the feedback they receive from others, good leaders invest time in reflecting on how they behaved and on how they *could* behave better in future similar circumstances. When you concentrate on the future in this way, you create a strong emotional marker for that improved behavior. Then, when you find yourself in a similar situation, your brain reminds you of that better behavior to use. Reflection time is one of the most worthwhile self-development habits you could implement.

Feedback + Reflection = Faster progress

How well do you understand you? For leaders advancing in their careers, understanding you can be one of the most important factors to keep your climb going.

Creating the Right Surround Sound

As a leader, you must know who to bring into your team. Knowing yourself well is a crucial part of being able to do that. If you have a good grasp on your strengths and weaknesses, you will recruit team leaders who have strength in your areas of weakness.

Leaders who surround themselves with people just like them are immature or ineffective. Staffing in this manner may magnify their strengths, but it simultaneously amplifies their weaknesses. Successful leaders build a diverse team of leaders, each of whom have strengths that complement those of the other team members. These leaders also embrace diversity in all forms; they know the more diverse input and discussions, the stronger the resulting solutions.

Diversity is even more important in larger organizations. The larger the organization you lead, the more your overall success is based on the combination of yours and your team's talents and achievements than it is your own. It's no secret that success is a team sport. If you look at past leaders of nations, you notice that those who were judged as lightweights can often achieve more than others because they built the right team around them, people who provide a good balance of abilities and experiences.

The leaders with whom you surround yourself are one of the most important factors in your quality of life. Your quality of life is in direct proportion to the level of teamwork and ownership the leaders around you take for the results of your team.

How is the quality of your surround sound (your leadership team)? Invest the time to grow a strong team and develop them to take more ownership of the team's achievements. You'll grow as a leader—and as a person.

Liked or Respected . . . or Both?

People often pose the question, *As a leader, do you want to be* liked *or* respected? (implying that it's not possible to achieve both). There are far too many leaders whose goal is to be liked. This desire often drives behaviors that don't lead to team success. This is why such leaders don't ask for feedback; they view any kind of criticism as a message that people don't like them.

Both are probably the right answer. However, leaders cannot always make the most popular decision. When you understand *you*, you can better control your emotions and make those important but occasionally unpopular decisions when they are needed most.

Embrace the Differences

If you lead across distances and cultures, every day you will encounter people who differ from you. People who understand themselves well have the confidence to embrace these differences. They're not afraid of people who aren't like them, nor do they avoid them. They know that differences are the norm in an international setting. They know that people who embrace those differences can enact stronger solutions and prompt better performance from their team. Leaders who avoid differences always struggle and often use differences as excuses as to why things didn't get done.

One international manager I know sees the distinctions in her team members as an advantage. She brings people together from different countries and different mind-sets to develop implementation plans, especially when kicking off new initiatives. This diverse input allows the plan to cover more of the unique issues that could slow down its implementation. It also saves the time it would take to resolve those issues in the middle of the process.

Being surrounded by diverse employees enables leaders to grow faster than if they are surrounded by people more like them. The more diverse the people you work with, the more you end up learning about yourself, which in turn helps you interact more effectively with even more different people! You must have the confidence to embrace the differences to gain all those advantages.

Deal with the Circumstances You Are Given

The more you know about yourself, the stronger you become in dealing with whatever arises in business or in life in general. Successful leaders, and especially leaders who deal with the complexity of distance and cultures, are expert at dealing with the circumstances they are given. They don't spend any time wishing things were difference or dwelling on how great it would be if they didn't have the problems they have. They simply just get on with it and deal with the problems they're facing.

Do you ever catch yourself saying, "I wish . . ."? The more you take the mind-set of just deal with it, the faster you get through it, whatever *it* is.

The more you understand you, the stronger the foundation of your influence and the greater your adaptability to use that influence.

Everything Starts with You Understanding You
(Takeaways)

- Your ability to understand yourself provides the foundation for you to better adapt to others.
- Distance magnifies behavior, so focus on bringing the best you each day.
- Requesting feedback from others and reflecting on your behavior is the fastest way to grow.

Your Key Reflection Questions

- Why did I behave that way, and how could I behave better in the future?
- Am I embracing the differences in others, or am I avoiding people who are different than me?
- Have I made both daily and weekly reflection a habit in my life?

5 Strengthening Your Character and Focus (Your Foundation)

The subject of character in leadership often drives a good debate among younger leaders, because they see so many who are "successful," yet whom others view as having a bad character and behavior. This naturally prompts them to ask, "So why is having a good character so important?" That's a great question.

Charisma might attract people, but your character keeps them with you. Because of that, character can be one of the most powerful aspects of your leadership, especially when you are leading across distances and cultures. People will often follow a leader because of who they are, and even if their direction is not entirely clear.

Charisma grabs attention; character grabs followers.

Who gives you more problems: the person with a lack of skill or the person with a lack of character? A lot of different elements comprise that thing we call character. Although it can seem vague at times, following are a few attributes of character that are crucial for leaders to display, especially those who lead across distances and cultures.

Attitude

A vital part of a leader's character is the attitude he or she brings to each and every moment of each and every day. The following story illustrates the importance of having the right attitude:

> An elderly woman was moving from one retirement home to another. As she was walking down the hallway of her new home, an attendant described her room to her, saying, "You have a beautiful view out into the courtyard, where there are trees and flowers.

You have plenty of room for your clothing. The room is nicely decorated, and you have a TV with all the different cultural channels to watch."

Before they reached the room, the elderly woman said, "I am going to love it."

The attendant looked at her strangely and asked, "How can you say that? You haven't even seen the room yet."

The woman answered, *"My attitude is something I determine ahead of time."*

Attitude is a choice—and successful leaders never surrender the leadership of their attitude to the team around them or others they meet throughout the day.

Successful leaders determine their attitude ahead of time.

You see why this is in the first few minutes of your meetings, especially the virtual meetings you hold. How you start the meetings and the focus you bring to what you want to accomplish will determine whether your people are going to be listening and participating or they are going to tune out you out while they check their e-mail.

If your attitude drops, your power of influence drops, too—and so does the power of your leadership.

Discipline and Commitment

You've probably never seen a successful leader who *wasn't* disciplined. Perhaps some leaders are mixed up at times, focusing on other parts of their lives. Successful leaders, however, are very disciplined in what drives their personal and team's success.

They've made it a habit to complete their nonenjoyable activities first, because they know this gets them closer to reaching their goals and that they will be setting the right example for others. It is crucial for those leading across distances and cultures to create and maintain credibility with their people. The way to keep your discipline, commitment, and credibility visible to your people is simple:

Say = Do

Your people notice consistency, and when you consistently deliver on what you say, your credibility rises. Across distances and cultures, your personal credibility drives your people to action, even when they might not clearly understand the why behind what they need to accomplish. They are doing it because of *you*, because you've demonstrated that for you, say = do.

Empathy: Responsible *to* versus *For*

Successful leaders are great listeners. They display the kind of empathy that shows their people that they care about them as individuals, not just resources. Being genuinely empathetic requires that you are actually *interested in* your people and interested in helping them achieve to their abilities. It's about helping your people find solutions to their problems. But it is *never* about you, their leader, taking your people's problems on as your own. It is about being responsible *to* versus responsible *for*. You cannot take responsibility for other people's lives; you can only be responsible *to* them—that is, help them be the best they can.

Responsible *to* drives the energy toward solutions.

Sadly, some leaders have the *to* and *for* the other way around, constantly taking on their people's problems. If you start feeling responsible for your people, slow down. When you slow down, you slow down your entire team. Leaders who are responsible *to* have empathy and are listening closely to their people. However, they think of only two things when employees bring problems to them: (1) What action can this team member take to solve the problem on his or her own? and (2) What action can I as a leader take do to support *his or her* action? This allows leaders to focus their energy entirely on finding a solution, and thus not allowing their people's negative energy to come to them.

How can you tell if you feel responsible *to* or *for* your people? The first involves a solution-oriented listening focus that encourages your people to solve more problems on their own and prevents you, their leader, from feeling that ownership, too.

You have likely heard the story about never letting your people transfer the monkey, or the problem, to you. One leader I know tells his staff, "You can bring the monkey to me. I will help you dress it, give it haircut, give it a shampoo . . . but the monkey leaves with you when you leave."

That's a great focus. The ownership for the problem always leaves with your people, and your responsibility is to help enable their actions for finding the solution.

Excellence, Especially in the Fundamentals

Effective leaders—in business, sports, and other realms—all operate according to one consistent theme: they focus on excellence and on the *fundamentals* that drive their team's success.

Common sense tells us that perfection is unattainable. However, successful leaders view perfection in the fundamentals as something to be pursued. They know that when the fundamentals are right, the results will be, too.

If you were to compare the practices of top teams in any sport to the bottom teams, you would notice some significant differences. Top teams' managers tend to focus on the fundamentals; they've usually created particular sequences in the practices that drill those fundamentals into their players. When game time comes, their players are repeating the fundamentals in their play automatically, without thinking.

It is the same with the very best leaders in business. They have such a strong focus on the fundamentals and know that these provide the foundation for greater speed and quality within their teams.

Do you know what the fundamentals are for your team's success?
As discussed in Chapter 1, good leaders are not micromanagers.
However, they do explore and hone in on the right *details* with their
people: the fundamentals.

$$- - - - - \text{Milestones} - -\text{M} - - - \text{M} \cdot - - \text{M} - - - - \blacktriangleright \text{Outcomes}$$
$$\text{and}$$
$$- - - - - \cdot \text{Fundamentals} - - - - - \cdot$$

These leaders know that when the fundamentals are in place, the
outcomes have a better chance of being precisely what they're
seeking.

Integrity

A great way to describe integrity is *the ability to guarantee all your
other qualities through your values and actions.* Having integrity
means that you're able to make consistent choices—you behave
consistently—and that consistency drives your people to follow you.

Integrity is even more important in a multicultural environment. The differences that exist among business and social customs
make it impossible to always do the "right thing" for each culture and in every situation. This is highlighted with the following
question:

*If two leaders make a cultural mistake, which one is forgiven faster:
the one with integrity or the one without?* People will always forgive a
person with integrity more easily and put the mistake out of their
mind. Leaders who lack this important quality aren't so lucky. People
don't forgive them or forget; they might even use the mistake to their
advantage in another situation.

Your integrity is what compels people to listen to you before you
even start speaking. It's also why they're willing to follow you before
they even fully understand the direction in which you are taking them.

Your Focus

Time management is always a hot topic; everyone wants to do more and achieve more in the same 24 hours. The truth is that you cannot manage time; everyone gets the same amount, and that's not going to change. In fact, the most common excuse bandied about—and the one with the least amount of credibility—is "I didn't have the time."

Successful leaders know that their focus drives their success, for themselves and for their teams. Rather than worrying about time management, it's *focus management*. They view their focus as the criteria for what they say yes and no to each day. So many priorities are competing with each other for leaders' focus and attention.

These leaders define their focus (their priorities) ahead of time and then compare the issues that arise during the day to their original focus. As we discussed in Chapter 1, unsuccessful and unfocused leaders tend to live in their inboxes, letting their teams and others drive their day. Successful and focused leaders live in their outboxes and are focused on the outcomes they are driving and on making progress. Their key criteria question is, *Is this helping me move my top priorities forward?*

Urgent - - - - - - *Compete with* - - - - - ▶ **Important**

Successful leaders force the urgent to compete with the important, not the other way around. They find their own unique way to keep the important in the front of their mind, which helps them better decide how to prioritize and *use* their time.

They also recognize that important is composed of the focus for both short- and long-term outcomes and achievements, and they realize that they can accomplish big changes and achievements for the future only through the actions they take today and every day.

Consider the following story:

A sculptor's assistant was bringing a big block of marble into the sculptor's studio. It was very dusty, dirty, and disfigured, and the assistant couldn't believe anything beautiful could be made out of something that looked so ugly. He said to the sculptor, "What are you going to make from this ugly piece of marble?"

The sculptor looked at it from every different angle and then finally said, "I see a magnificent, muscular stallion, with flowing mane and flared nostrils."

The assistant asked, "But, how are you going to make it?"

"I am going to take my hammer and my chisel, and I am going to chip away, and chip away, and chip away everything that is not a horse; and what's left over will be a masterpiece."

(chip away) | — Focus — | *(chip away)*

To remain truly focused, you need to be constantly chipping away—in other words, saying no—to the things that keep you from being your best, achieving your masterpiece, and helping your team do the same.

Saying no more often actually makes your yes stronger each time you use it. Remember what we learned in Chapter 1: you either make your choice or by default allow others to make your choice for you. If you are not focused as a leader, then you're allowing others outside your team to drive you.

One Final Word on What You Don't Need to Know

Success used to be about what you *know*. Today, success is more difficult to pin down. It's about finding the right balance between establishing what you need to know and working out how you can use it to take action and achieve and more experience, without slowing down the decision-making process.

Effective leadership is easier to achieve when we determine from the very start what it is we really *need to know* to take action today and what we need to know long term to ensure we make better choices in the future. We need to build that foundation of knowledge that allows us to better use our instincts. It helps us make more informed choices, take more effective action, and achieve more as a result.

So ask yourself, *What don't you really need to know?* And what do you *absolutely* need to know to meet your own and your team's current and future goals? Once you've determined that, everything else is simply a nice to know. When you focus on what you need to know, you free up both your time and energy for you and your team to take more action on the important issues.

Remember, you are the role model for your team. Character and focus create a good role model for your people.

Strengthening Your Character and Focus (Your Foundation) (Takeaways)

- Charisma attracts people to you, but your character keeps them with you.
- Be disciplined to do what's needed when it is necessary.
- Create and maintain your focus, and force the urgent to compete with the important.

Your Key Reflection Questions

- On a scale of 1 to 10, how is my attitude today? Remember, a 10 is just a choice!

- Have my behaviors been consistent with my words? Is what I *say* equal to what I *do?*

- Have I forced the urgent to compete with the important?

6 Keeping Your Perspective and Balancing Your Stress

A high-potential leader was discussing with his mentor the difficulty he was having managing the ever-increasing expectations of his boss and the management. He found it difficult to maintain his focus and his perspective on what needed to be done. His mentor recounted some advice he had received years prior: "Leadership success is often enabled by how we deal with that little voice in our head that we can't do something or we aren't good enough."

Everyone has that voice, and stress often magnifies its volume. It causes us to lose perspective on our work *and* in our personal lives. It can be easy to lose your perspective when you're facing the challenges of leading across distances and cultures. The complexity often drives you to chase people down for what they are responsible for delivering, and you're frequently dealing with cross-country politics. Whatever you can do to help keep the right perspective will allow you to be the right role model for your people and prompt you to make the right decisions to keep it moving in the right direction.

Think about what happens when you lose your perspective. You become more stressed, it gets harder to focus, and you end up losing energy. You also start to think less clearly. That's because stress results in:

1. *Less blood getting to your brain.* The human body functions in a certain—and not always beneficial—way. When you're under stress, it expects you to do physical work, and more blood goes to your arms and legs . . . and away from your brain. Only in recent years has work become more mental.

2. *Your lower brain taking over more.* You have three parts to your brain, and when you're under stress, the lower part of the

77

brain—that which is linked to survival—kicks in. Unfortunately, this isn't the high-level thinking part of the brain.

It's clear that stress affects your perspective. Reduced thinking ability, decreased focus, and loss of energy come at the detriment of your leadership effectiveness and impact.

With stress being people's biggest and most frequently cited problem, the key is to manage the stress and not let it manage *you*. How do you do that? It's about *drinking down* the stress, but not in the way you think. It's not about grabbing that pint of beer or that glass of wine to relieve your stress. There are other, much more beneficial ways to do this.

We'll use a glass of water as our analogy; water represents the stress that can pour into your life. As your stress grows, more water is being poured into the glass. If water continues to be added, it will eventually overflow. That's usually when stress drives you to do or say something you wish you hadn't. And that action may affect your relationship with a team member. When this happens across locations and cultures, it may even take months to recover to the same level of trust that you had before.

Gap

Stress

Successful leaders who manage stress well don't necessarily have low *levels* of stress. In fact, their stress levels can be quite high. Think of their glasses as being two-thirds full all the time. But these leaders have found ways to either stop the flow (the pouring of more water) or reduce the amount of stress they are carrying by drinking the water down. If you live your life with stress always at the top of the glass, every little problem can drive you to react with in ways that negatively affect both *your* perspective and the perception others will have of you.

There are ways to stop the flow of stress and reduce the amount you carry. This is something experts call your recovery. And the way you create your recovery time has a big impact on your ability to handle stress and keep your perspective.

1. To Stop the Flow of Stress: Break the Pattern

The initial goal is to stop the stress from building. Usually this doesn't take a great deal of time, and it's simple to do. When you find the stress level rising during your day:

- Take a quick coffee break. (Get out of the office and stop by the local café.)
- Listen to your favorite song. (It takes your mind to another place.)
- Picture yourself enjoying your last holiday or even look at photos from your last holiday. (It creates a different feeling.)

One executive takes a 5-minute walk around the block when his stress starts to increase. This very quick break alters the pattern of the stress and keeps it from continuing to build. It also provides a little fresh air and thinking time.

All stress control requires is a change in your mind-set or a small action that will break your current pattern of thought and thereby alter your feelings. If you can stop that flow from building within you, then you have broken the pattern!

2. Reduce the Amount of Stress You Are Carrying: Recharge the Batteries

Reducing the amount of stress you carry requires that you incorporate activities into your life that will drink down the water in the glass. This will make room for you to handle the additional stress that will inevitably come. Some options are:

- Visit your health club. (The endorphins always make you feel better.)
- Have dinner with friends. (It takes you mind away from the stress.)
- Go for a run. (The combination of exercise and being outside helps clear the mind.)
- Call a close friend for a chat. (Talking with others releases our stress.)

People who manage their stress well also do something specific that makes all the difference: they plan these activities *each week*. Each week, they look at their calendar and determine which days will be most stressful. Then they decide what activities—or stress busters— they can plug into their calendar that will ease some of this burden.

These are just a few ideas. The most important thing is for you to understand what activities work best to both break the pattern and reduce the amount of stress you are carrying around.

So figure it out now, before you need it. *What are your favorite recovery activities? Which ones work best for you?* If you can determine in advance how to manage your stress, stress will never manage you again—or cause you to say the wrong thing at the wrong time!

Think Ahead and Keep Your Focus

The other important part of keeping your perspective is to keep your focus. Losing it usually means that you're letting the urgent overtake the important. This will filter down to your people, who will then begin to focus on and do the same.

The more time you block off to invest in and reconfirm your focus, the more progress you make on the important—and the more you say no to the unimportant urgent. Successful leaders schedule their thinking time when they are in great shape, when their clarity of thinking is at their best. For some that will be mornings; for others, afternoons or evenings. Some will even thrive very late at night and into the early hours of the morning.

One leader who understood the importance of thinking time would take a poll of his leaders to see when their best times were. The majority said it was their mornings, so the leader scheduled all the important operational and strategy meetings in the morning. He then moved all the routine meetings to the afternoons.

Do you know your best times . . . when you are most productive? What about your people's? When do you schedule meetings for your team?

The Stories You Tell Yourself

When you think about it, your perspective is really based on the stories you tell yourself about what has happened in your day/week. The leaders who maintain a good perspective and keep taking action are always telling themselves a forward-thinking story.

What stories are you telling yourself? The more you are aware of them, the more you can change them to ones that empower you. The stories you tell yourself can make all the difference.

Keeping Your Perspective and Balancing Your Stress
(Takeaways)

- Balance your stress with some type of recovery to keep your stress glass from always being full.

- Make your recovery and thinking time a priority that you protect.

- Plan in advance to confirm your focus and to keep your thinking ahead of your team.

Your Key Reflection Questions

- Have I protected my recovery and thinking time for the coming week?

- What recovery activities work best in helping me keep the right perspective?

- Do the stories I am telling myself (my inner chatter) paint a positive picture?

Part III
Influencing Others (Enabling Personal Ownership)

An old saying describes leadership as *simply influence*. It is about influencing others in ways that align within your own self-interest—and getting people to do and achieve what you want them to.

The goal is to have employees take ownership for the both their and the team's achievements and to constantly be seeking solutions to any problems that get in their way. The more you can convince people to own their achievement, the more control you will have over your team. Real control comes through leading people, not managing activities.

Over time, you will see how developing key people enhances your ability to influence your entire team, as well as others throughout the company.

Influencing Others: Enabling Personal Ownership Chapters

7 Investing in Your Key People (The Extension of You)

If you gain influence by managing people, then you extend that influence by developing the key people on your team, the individuals with whom you regularly surround yourself. Your success is directly linked to your their success, so the more successful you enable *them* to be, the more successful *you* will be.

One international executive in a global consumer business viewed the forming of his leadership team as one of his most important priorities. He knew that the individuals he chose would essentially determine his team's ability to deliver the performance his boss was seeking. He made his first priority to fill the most important roles in his leadership team with strong people, people who could then serve as role models for the others. It took time to find the right people for these positions; some who observed him thought he was going too slowly and questioned why he wasn't looking to fill all the roles as fast as he could. But taking such a focused and methodical approach allowed this leader to find and hire the role models he needed to extend his influence—and build a far stronger leadership team.

Your key people are the most important members of your team. They are an extension of you, and their behavior and leadership drive team performance when you're absent. The most successful leaders focus more of their time with their key people than with the others. They know that these individuals are the role models who help create and reinforce the right behaviors throughout your organization and are their partners in developing a culture of success.

You might be wondering whether it's fair to not give *all* your people equal time and attention. Fair is never a good achievement goal.

Fair isn't objective; everyone has a different perception of what *fair* is. Consistency is a much better achievement goal. Investing more in your most critical team members simply means that you're being consistent with their importance to the team with the energy you expend on their development.

So, who *are* your key people? The best way to identify them is to analyze both performance and behavior, plotting people on scale as shown here:

Low ◀ - - - - - - - - | - - - - - - - - ▶ High

Performance (P) is measured by how well your people deliver to expectations

Behavior (B) is measured by how well your people live your organiztion's values and work with others

Here are some examples of how you could use this scale.

High in Performance and Behavior (Your Key People and Focus)

People high in performance and behavior are the ones who are driving your team's success. They are the extension of you when you are not in the office and the role models for the rest of your team.

P

Low ◀ - - - - - - - - | - - - - - - - - ▶ High

B

Successful leaders focus on developing these people first, and then ask these people to develop others, particularly those who are either low in performance or low in behavior. Those people who are low in both areas require an approach described later in this chapter.

Key people can help you drive change within your team, and it's important to continually challenge them with projects that will help grow their business judgment.

High in Performance, Low in Behavior

People high in performance but low in behavior are often some of the most difficult people to deal with. They do a lot of good work, but they don't live the values of the team or work well with others.

This is often seen in sales teams. You have star performers who achieve great results by using (and sometimes abusing) others in the team, particularly the support people. Very often, you have a situation where customers love this person, but he or she is driving chaos within your team with his or her behavior.

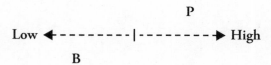

Coaching can sometimes be effective with these people. But if they don't change and are preventing collaboration within your team, you have to get them out. Resistance to collaboration hinders developing better solutions, which slows the overall progress of your team's performance.

Low in Performance, High in Behavior

People who are low in performance but high in behavior often get along well with others, but tend to be individuals who don't like to take personal ownership, resulting in their poor performance.

$$\text{P}$$
Low ◀ – – – – – – – | – – – – – – – ▶ High
$$\text{B}$$

It's vital to learn more about the root causes of these individuals' poor performance; some can be addressed with additional training and mentoring. If this is the case, having them work with team members on small projects could help grow their skills and performance faster. However, you might unearth some root causes that lead you to think that this person may not be a good long-term fit for this role.

Low in Performance, Low in Behavior

This is where leaders have to focus on with the support of human resources (HR). These people are both not performing to expectations and are not getting along well with others.

$$\text{P}$$
Low ◀ – – – – – – – | – – – – – – – ▶ High
$$\text{B}$$

Successful leaders give these people one or two chances, and if they don't improve, they're out. This might sound harsh, but there are two reasons for this: (1) If you don't do something about these people, you will disappoint your key people the most. They will continue to have to work with these individuals, all while expecting you to have done something about their unsatisfactory performance and unprofessional behavior. (2) You are doing bottom performers a disservice if you don't try to help them move to a role that's better suited for them. Their abilities are clearly not matching to this role, and as their leader, the best you can do is to help them find one that does.

This performance/behavior assessment is a great way to see who your key people are and determine how to use them to develop others. This process constantly supports and enhances your team's abilities and performance.

Why not invest time this week to mark where your people on this performance/behavior assessment? There are three key questions to ask yourself if determining where to mark them:

1. How does their performance compared with your communicated expectations?

2. How well are they living the communicated values and principles of the team?

3. Are they able to be a team player in the key times when their help is needed?

Your People Feel Challenged to Solve It First

There's a great way to evaluate whether you have the right people around you, the kind who will take ownership for what they are doing: they'll always feel challenged to solve a problem first, before bringing it to you.

The right people exhibit strengths in the areas where you are asking them to do work. They feel confident to take on challenges without always coming back to you for answers or advice. You can always tell if a challenge is outside a person's strengths; that's when they take the easy approach by returning to you for an answer.

The right people also show that they have and want ownership for the problem *and* solution when they try to resolve it on their own. They'll also put more energy into the execution.

When do your people bring problems to you? This question's answer is indicative of the level of ownership your team is taking for achievement. If they bring the problems to you before trying to come up with their own solution, it's a sign that you have an ownership issue within your team.

Successful leaders always ask their team members to come—right from the beginning—with possible solutions or options to discuss. They know that using a solution that includes their people's input will always compel the team to take more ownership of the solution.

Focus on Their Strengths and Their Most Important Weakness

Your people's strengths are what make them successful, so you should focus the bulk of your development on enhancing these strengths. Unfortunately, many leaders take the opposite approach: they concentrate on developing their people's weaknesses.

There are essentially two types of weaknesses: (1) those that keep people from fully using their strengths and (2) those that have no impact on their ability to use their strengths. The focus for number 2 should be on surrounding your people with others who have strengths in the areas where they're lacking; for example, a salesperson might lack financial analysis skills that could be provided by support person. If you're dealing with a weakness of type 1, you must focus on developing that *one* weakness that is preventing your people from using their strengths to the fullest.

For the majority of people, this *one* weakness is usually related to some type of communication or influencing skill. The employee is often very skilled at a particular area of the business but lacks the ability to get other people to adopt his or her ideas or help in their implementation.

For leaders, there is often one communication behavior that impacts their leadership success more than any other: their listening. One leader of an R&D team in a start-up company realized that his one weaknesses of not listening was stopping some good ideas from progressing. With the help of his mentor, he realized that his own mind-set was discounting his people's ideas before they ever had the chance to fully explain them.

Strengths ◀- - - - - - - - - Weaknesses with Impact (1)

Weaknesses without Impact (2)

If you consider the 80/20 rule, you see that your people grow faster when you devote 80 percent of the development to growing their strengths, and 20 percent to working on that one most glaring weakness.

How can you make feedback on weaknesses a positive discussion? The best way is to *never* discuss a weakness by itself, in isolation. Start by discussing the employee's strengths and complimenting that person on what's been done well. You can then touch on how this strength could be enhanced even further if the person concentrated on improving whatever weakness is holding him or her back. This approach lets you package the weaknesses with the strength and turn the conversation into something positive—specifically, by offering a way for the employee to grow and use his or her strengths even *more*.

One word to the wise about providing feedback: never bring up a weakness for the first time during a person's yearly appraisal discussion. Doing so causes you lose a great deal of credibility; your people are apt to wonder, "Why didn't my boss tell me about this sooner? I could have been working on this weakness, instead of having him hold it against me in determining my future at the company." And that reaction is spot on. You *should* be discussing areas for improvement sometime during the year—and more important, closer to the time you saw the behaviors that highlighted the weakness.

People can tell a great deal about you as a leader based on who you choose to have as part of your leadership team. If the people around you are just like you, you're letting everyone know about the holes you've created in your group's capabilities. When everyone is like you, you multiply your strengths (which is good), but unfortunately, you do the same for your weaknesses (which is very bad). In fact, stocking a leadership team with people just like you tells your boss that you are not really ready to lead.

If you are a leader who is very strategically oriented, surrounding yourself with the same type of people will often leave you and your team missing some important operational deadlines. As you all are big-picture people, you are not focused or motivated to ensure the details are correct. That's why all successful strategically oriented leaders surround themselves with great operational leaders/managers who are interested in getting the operational details right.

If you are a very practical manager, focused on day-to-day results, and surround yourself the same type of managers, you might end up missing some great opportunities. With such a strong day-to-day focus, you don't look at the operations through an innovative lens and miss opportunities that could make steep changes in the team's performance. Getting leaders around you who love challenging that status quo will help you look above the day-to-day work to see new opportunities.

There's another simple but very effective technique in evaluating whether you have the right people on staff. Make two columns on a piece of paper. Label the left column "strengths" and the right column "weaknesses":

◀ - - - - - Strengths - - - - - - | - - - - - - Weaknesses - - - - - ▶

Now pick a person on your team and start filling in the columns.

Whichever column you start writing in first will tell you a great deal about the person. Whatever you think of first—a strength or a weakness—will tell you everything you need to know. If your pen goes to the strengths column first, you are thinking about the strengths that help you and your team to be more successful. If your pen goes to the weaknesses column first, you are probably thinking of some type of behavior from this individual that is always stopping your team from performing better together and achieving better results.

Providing Feedback: Encouraging Your People to *Own* Their Improvement

It's important to emphasize a few key points about giving feedback on strengths and weaknesses, particularly when conducting performance appraisals. You want your people feeling motivated to improve and change. And you can encourage this by using one of the most underutilized leadership techniques available: *potential*.

How often do you talk with your people about their potential? Discussing what they could accomplish and what their next career steps might be is incredibly motivating. Unfortunately, many leaders limit their conversations about potential to once or twice a year—and that's a mistake. If you're going to inspire your people to do achieve and develop more, discussing potential once or twice a year is nowhere near enough.

Successful leaders make a habit of talking to their people about their potential. Throughout the year they plant the seeds, discussing with people what they are capable of, and then continually water those seeds in their more formal personal development discussions. The power of talking potential really shows up when you start delegating difficult outcomes to your people. Let's say you delegate something really difficult to James, one of your key people, but you never talk to him about his potential. James might be thinking, my leader is dumping on me again.

However, let's say that you have been continually dropping those seeds and talking with James about the potential throughout the year, indicating to him where he needs to develop and the type of responsibilities that would help him develop in those areas. Then, when you begin to delegate something difficult to James, he welcomes it because it's helping him grow his potential.

How Are Your One-on-Ones with Your People?

One-on-one meetings can tend to sneak up on many leaders, rendering them unprepared and unsure of what to cover. When not prepared, leaders often spend too much time on the latest operational issues, something that could be addressed through e-mail.

|------- Person ------ or ------ Operations ------|

What percentage of your one-on-one time with your people—especially key people—do you spend on discussing operations versus their professional development? Most give only about 10 percent to the person and 90 percent to the operations. If that's the case, how do you think that makes your people feel? The most successful leaders know that motivation is a feeling—and it's why they invest more of their one-on-one employee times discussing people's development. They know that when you invest in your people's success, they return the sentiment by making more of an investment in the team's success.

Think about how investing more in your people's success during your own one-on-one meetings can make a big difference to your people's investment in your team's success. For leaders who don't think there is enough time to do this, you can focus on getting multiple wins from the same conversation. If you focus the conversation on the team's outcomes you want achieved (win #1), you get your people focused on achievement and not just their own activities. Ask them how their own individual outcomes contribute to the team's outcomes, and you get them seeing how their success contributes to the team's success (win #2). Talk about future opportunities and ask how they see themselves contributing, and you can then ask them how they think they need to develop themselves to make those contributions even stronger (win #3). Successful leaders focus development conversations in the direction of achieving the team's outcomes.

Setting Expectations

One of the most important factors for monitoring your key people's growth is the way you set expectations for them. The expectations you set for them are really *team* expectations, because they're the role models for your team's performance. The expectations should be a stretch, but do-able, and should challenge your key people and your team to look for new and better ways to complete tasks and achieve goals.

Understanding and explaining the expectations that need to be set—and at what level—is a leadership skill. The way you get your key people and your team to reach their potential is to set expectations that compel them to use it.

You can create the right expectations in the form of challenges that drive your key people and your team to raise their game. Those might come from opportunities in your market, a competitor that is creating a problem for you, or a new product or service that could be a game changer for your team and company if you exploit it.

How far a stretch are the expectations you are giving to your key people? Are they forcing them to use their own and the team's potential? If you invest the time to create the right expectations for your key people, those people often have the power to bring your entire team to new levels of performance.

Get Your Key People Mentors

It's very difficult to give your key people the attention that they really deserve when leading across distances and cultures. Finding mentors for your key people can help in several ways.

For one thing, your people will receive great advice from someone who's been there and done that. Mentors have been in their shoes and understand what they're experiencing; they can provide what people need most in order to move forward and grow faster. The very practical advice that they have to offer will grow your people's skills and confidence faster.

Second, your people might feel comfortable sharing things in their discussions with their mentor that they would never have shared with their boss. Often, these are the very discussions that help your people change mind-sets and drive more action, both in terms of personal development and team performance.

Getting your key people mentors can greatly improve the pace at which they develop their careers and their business judgment. The faster they do the latter, the faster you can delegate more decisions to them.

Bring in HR as Your Partner

Because your success is really based on people, it is important to always bring HR in as your partner in your strategic initiatives. First, you always need to hire new people to join your team, especially if your company is growing and more is expected of your team. You will want to hire the best people you can, and a strong partnership with HR will help you do that. As the saying goes,

Hiring success is all about hiring people better than you.

When you do this, you always end up with better team performance. You get a replacement faster, so you can rise faster.

As with any team, there are some people who just won't perform to your expectations. You will have to find these people a new home or let them go. HR can help you do this, not only in the proper and legal way, but faster than might otherwise be possible.

Think of HR's importance in this way: you always have to do what's right for your people and be flexible with the way you treat them. You don't want to be doing the work that HR could be doing when your objective is to lead and manage your team. Always bring HR in as your partner and do so as early as possible.

Growing More Leaders

When you focus on your key people, you are growing more leaders. For your team to do and achieve more, you need your key people to act as role models for others, be willing to take ownership, and make decisions. And you would like at least *one* of them to be able to step up and take on your role in the future as well. You could summarize your role as a leader to grow more leaders. The more people with strong leadership skills in your team, the stronger your team becomes overall.

Investing in Your Key People (The Extension of You)
(Takeaways)

- Your key people are your team's role models when you are not there.
- Focus on and have your key people develop other team members.
- Concentrate primarily on your people's strengths and only one weakness to help use their strengths better.

Your Key Reflection Questions

- How much of my time do I focus on developing my key people?
- How often do I reinforce the strengths in my people (especially my key people)?
- Am I including HR and getting their help in developing my key people faster?

8 Delegating Outcomes and Asking Open Questions

One of the most difficult changes for leaders to make is learning to let go and delegate responsibilities to the people they manage. Many are used to doing it all and reluctant to let someone else take care of things. Some think their people will never do the job as well as they could. Others worry, "If I delegate this to my people, then what will *I* do?" That's a revealing question. If someone is worried that they won't have anything to do, then they see their job simply as doing other people's jobs! What and how you delegate reveals a great deal about the kind of leader you are to others—more than you think it might!

Successful leaders discuss and delegate outcomes. A focus on results requires that you speak in the language of achievement and encourage your people to take ownership of these outcomes.

If you delegate an activity to your people, who owns the outcome it supports? You do. Either the leader does, or no one does. Delegating an activity means delegating work, but not *achievement*. Successful leaders also ask their people to specify the milestones for achieving these outcomes. Your people will take far more ownership in milestones *they give you* than in anything you assign to them. In this way, delegating outcomes is really a double win for you as a leader:

1. You encourage your people to own an achievement and take the responsibility to make decisions and actions to make it happen.

2. Delegating outcomes to your people, especially new staff, helps you develop them faster. Training provides a foundation for development, but there is nothing that develops people faster than actually *doing it*.

You have to fight the urge to answer your people's questions. The more answers you give, the less overall influence you can have within your team.

Consider the following scenario: You are having a conversation with one of your people in your team. The person in your team is asking all the questions, and you are giving him or her all the answers.

Who controls the conversation? Clearly, it's not you; it's the person in your team. Now, if that is true, and if you are a leader who is answering your people's questions all day long, then that means that they are in control of every conversation with you!

Is that good? Probably not . . . Every time you provide an answer to your people's questions when you could have asked some questions of them to help them find their own answers, you have saved them from thinking.

If you save them from thinking, you save them from growing.

This is important. If you give your people the easy way out by giving them the answer—and thereby preventing them from figuring it out themselves—they will take that easy way every chance they get. And they'll keep coming back to *you* for all the answers.

The Power of Questions

Your power as a leader doesn't come from the answers but from the questions—because your questions:

1. Force your people to *think*.

2. Give your people a *thought process* to follow, which they can use for the next problem they face.

3. Allow your people to *own their answers* (versus relying on your answers).

Of course, you can't always avoid giving an answer. The key is to strike the right balance to drive more ownership in your people.

How was your balance of questions versus answers this past week? How you handle your people's questions drives their behaviors, either good or bad.

What Options Do We Have?

Successful leaders know that your people take more ownership in delivering their own ideas than others'. Instead of just providing solutions, they encourage the people they manage to come up with an answer. However, *how* a leader asks for the answer is just as important—if not more so—than encouraging ownership in the first place.

How often do you approach a scenario by asking your people, "What is the best thing to do here?" It's a common way to pose a question, but it doesn't necessarily get the best results. When you only ask for one thing and you don't happen to like it, you then need to convince your people to do something different. Now, the answer is no longer their answer but yours, decreasing their ownership in it.

The best way to ask is, *"What options do we have?"* Now, you get to coach your people toward what could be the best answer— and they keep the ownership, because *they* were the source of that answer.

This is especially important when managing teams that span distances and cultures. There are often very strong politics involved in coming up with the right solutions in these situations. At times, your people might not understand the politics involved and suggest something that might not be implementable given the politics involved. By having your people provide multiple solutions, it makes it easier to direct them away from these options and toward ones with less politics involved.

What You Ask about Comes about

One key leadership principle is centered on the questions you ask, because what you ask about comes about. Your questions' power lies in their quality. Your people will know that what you're asking about is important to you. Therefore, your people will know to pay attention to the questions you ask about outcomes (achievement) and to think how they are going to accomplish them (milestones). If, on the other hand, you barrage them with questions about every activity, they'll feel the need to report every activity to you, because they think you want to know *every little thing* that's going on.

One of the most crucial things for leaders to ask about is principles and values. It's yet another way to let your people know that you feel these are important.

Delegate What You Like Doing

Let's face it: every leader wants and prefers to delegate those annoying tasks and chores they don't like doing. It feels great to get rid of that work, and there's usually someone on the team who can do it better. However, *real* delegation comes when you begin delegating the activities you like doing, things you should probably be letting go of anyway. If you are leading a growing team, you'll often find that you need to continually define your role as that team grows. The things you were good at and enjoyed doing last year may not be something you should—or want to—be doing this year. As a your team grows, you also have to grow, and that means letting go of some things you enjoyed doing in order to take on new challenges.

You impede the growth of two key elements by keeping hold of the same responsibilities for too long:

1. *Your key people:* You prevent them from growing by not delegating those things to them.

2. *Your team:* By continuing to do those things, you might not be seeing some opportunities to grow your team's performance even more.

So think about it: *Are there things you enjoy doing that you should be letting go of today?* Remember, your people, especially your key people, notice what you hold on to. And they'll be disappointed that you are not delegating those jobs and helping them grow.

Recognizing Contribution

People want to make a difference. They want to know that their work is contributing to something important. Therefore, you must always reinforce the contributions your people are making. Linking these to the team's underlying why is crucial, whether you do it during one-on-one or group meetings.

The most successful leaders recognize their employees' work in a variety of ways, recognizing all different sizes of contributions. True recognition is not a one-time event; it's a *habit*, or a set of habits. The more creative your methods for recognizing contribution are, the more motivated your people will be to find more creative solutions.

A few ways to recognize contribution are:

- Writing a simple handwritten note to your people when you notice their great work (it's personal and often kept for a long time by your people)

- Mentioning their contribution in meetings with other departments (word always gets back to them on what you said)

- Providing a gift certificate for something your people's families can enjoy too (extend your people's pride to their entire life)
- Creating a practice within the team to celebrate together a key contribution from one of the team members (links personal and team contributions together)

Growing Business Judgment

If you do not trust your employees' business judgment, you certainly won't delegate decisions to them. You need to know how sound your people's business judgment is; if you don't have confidence in it, you keep more decisions at your level than you really should. You grow your people's business judgment by giving them a variety of responsibilities, experiences, and training with others outside your company. It is this combination of initiatives, as well as your people's own personal development, that grows their ability to make sound business decisions.

This is where the art of leadership comes into play. People *grow when they are uncomfortable*, when they're taking on new challenges or experiences. Effective leaders are able to judge how uncomfortable they can make their people while making sure they're still strong and confident enough to keep taking action. You might phrase it as encouraging them to be comfortable being a *little* uncomfortable.

The key is determining just how much discomfort they can take and still remain productive and growth-oriented. Leaders often complain about the difficult decisions that they need to make, which I find strange. After all, a leader's primary goal is to grow their people's business judgment. If that's what a leader has been doing, then his or her people should be making most of the decisions—only the most difficult should ever reach the leader.

So think about it: *What could you delegate to grow your key people's business judgment?* Remember, you need to delegate outcomes instead of activities to get your people to own achievement. It is only by delegating outcomes that you can also delegate the decisions that will help grow your people's business judgment faster.

For some important meetings, why not let your people not only do the preparation for the meetings but also lead the meetings. When you let your people take ownership for the outcomes and make them visible to others in the company, you get a double win: your people take on more ownership for results, and others in the company gain trust in.

Delegation is part skill and part art. The skill comes in knowing *what* to delegate. The art is knowing *when and how* you can stretch your people while ensuring that they still have the confidence to take action on their own.

One successful leader developed a list of potential outcomes he could delegate to key people if the opportunities arose in the future. He selected opportunities he believed would expand people's knowledge and experiences, creating a foundation for strong business judgment. When these outcomes came up to delegate, the leader used his already-prepared list to make an instant match.

If you don't think ahead and prepare possible outcomes to delegate to your key people, you'll likely overlook these opportunities or think of them too late, thereby failing to give your people the proper time to achieve those outcomes in a successful way. If you miss opportunities to delegate, you are slowing down your team's development—and eventual success.

Remember that although training provides a foundation, delegation is the fastest way to develop your people. Encouraging, and in some cases, forcing them to take on new challenges and opportunities is what really develops your people *and* their business judgment.

Delegating Outcomes and Asking Open Questions
(Takeaways)

- Delegating is the fastest way to grow your people.

- Ask more questions rather than giving answers; never save your people from thinking.

- True delegation starts when you delegate what you like to do.

Your Key Reflection Questions

- How was my combination of questions and answers this past week?

- Am I holding on to something I like doing, thereby preventing my people from growing?

- Have I identified the right responsibilities and experiences to grow business judgment in my key people?

9 Getting Others to Think, Feel, and Do (The Outcome of Communication)

There's a scene from a movie I like in which a teacher is explaining the story behind a famous painting to her students. None of the children are really listening to what she is saying. She wonders how to get their attention; then she asks the class, "Do you know this painting is worth $5 million?" Suddenly, every child is silent and hooked on her every word.

Very often, good communication starts by simply getting others *to want to listen* to what you have to say. If people don't *want* to listen, you'll have a difficult time getting them to hear—let alone *understand*—what you have to say.

A leader's communications skills and capacity to build rapport quickly and communicate clearly has a direct impact on that leader's ability to influence others—something we know by now *every* effective leader can do.

Consider this question: *Is communication an activity or an outcome?* People usually tend to see it as an activity, or some combination of both. The *act* of communicating is purely an activity, but in many teams, it is *an activity with the hope of an outcome.* The reason you are communicating lies in what you are trying to achieve.

The Outcome of Communication

The real outcome of communication comes down to three words. It is all about getting others to:

Think

Feel

Do

You want people to think a certain way, to feel a certain way, and to take some type of action.

When it comes to encouraging your people to take action, getting them to feel a certain way has a much greater impact then getting them to think a certain way. Motivation is more of a *feeling* than a thought.

Strategic Patience: When to Really Listen

Are successful leaders patient or impatient? It's an interesting question to consider. People often say that successful leaders are *patient*. However, let's say you tell your bosses that you are a day or two behind on a particular project. Are they likely to respond by telling you not to worry and to take an extra week? I don't think so. Successful leaders are *impatient*. They want everything done yesterday. They're focused on achieving the goals and getting there as fast as they can.

However, they also display something I call *strategic patience*. For example, they know when to just sit and listen an extra 10 minutes in order to have people leave a meeting with the right feeling to take more action. They know that they get people to feel by how they listen.

During a 360 review, one research-and-development (R&D) leader in a high-tech company received feedback indicating that he doesn't listen. This is normal with very successful leaders who want everything done yesterday—and that impatience led this leader to always try to cut his conversations with his people short. He basically focused on telling his employees what they needed to know, nothing more. With some coaching he realized that he had to learn how to display *strategic patience*. He had to listen to cues to determine when his employees wanted to talk through a problem or solution. As he began to read these cues more successfully and listen more, he found that his people were leaving discussions with more confidence—and taking more effective action as well. When he took the extra time to listen *at the right time*, his people felt more confident and empowered and began to make more decisions and take more action on their own.

Strategic patience is essential for leading across distances and cultures. You need your people to have the confidence to make decisions and take action without continually coming back to you.

Successful leaders know when to just stop and listen.

If you're asking your people to do something quite difficult and you don't invest the time to listen to how they're going to go about achieving it, then they feel that you really don't know what it's going to take for them to complete that difficult assignment. If, however, you take the time to listen, they feel that their boss understands how difficult the assignment will be. As a result, they're more empowered and motivated to make it happen.

The Power of Stories and Examples

The use of stories and examples helps leaders bring alive in others' minds what they are trying to communicate. They incite emotion in others, which makes your communications far more memorable.

One speaker/trainer often asks this question midway through his session: *How would today be if I never told you a single story or never gave you a single example?* The group usually responds by telling him that the presentation would be boring, not relevant, and just theory—that it would have less impact.

Your leadership communications work the same way. If you are not using stories and examples to illustrate your key messages, then you probably aren't having the right impact! Stories and examples bring to life what you are trying to say. They compel people to pay attention and listen to understand how the story ends. A long explanation simply causes your people to lose concentration and possibly miss the most important part of your message.

Stories and examples are also very powerful in international teams. Although the common business language is usually English, not everyone speaks or understands English at the same level—or expresses himself or herself in the same way. Stories allow people to understand the concepts you want to highlight, even when there's a slight language barrier, and people can often fill in words they might miss in the information you share. Take a cue from successful speakers: they usually tell stories, and they do so in succession, while sharing just a few bits of information in between. They know that their audience will pay attention to hear how the story ends rather than lose concentration in the middle of a long explanation.

Stories and examples are also *memorable*. If what you say is not memorable, then it is not *transferable*. Your communication goes no further than the person you're talking with unless you can make it memorable.

What are the stories and examples that can make your communications more memorable? You can use stories and examples from your own career or from your personal development (from the books you have read or the audio you have listened to). The more stories and examples you have, the more opportunities to pick the one that will be the most meaningful and memorable for a particular situation.

5-Minute Conversations

Offices are full of 5-minute conversations. When you're leading people based in the same office, these conversations are easy enough to have. You stop someone in the hallway, drop by someone's desk, or grab a coffee together. However, you often lose that opportunity when you're leading virtual teams across distances and cultures. Members of these kinds of teams more often send one another e-mails or use instant messaging to deal with smaller issues in real time. They often lack the ability to have short conversations that can resolve issues more quickly—or even just plant the seeds of alignment that enable you to move much faster on a matter in the future.

Some people even claim that social media has killed the 5-minute chat. But the best teams are still willing to pick up the phone and call someone to get the benefit of that 5-minute conversation. Fostering this behavior can be difficult, because people are naturally reluctant to bother their seemingly always busy colleagues. But if you're merely relying on an exchange of e-mails or formal meetings and Web conferencing to resolve issues, you won't tackle problems as quickly or effectively as your office-based counterparts can.

The willingness to pick up the phone, address an issue, and maybe talk about an opportunity helps teams move much faster.

But how do you encourage this? One way is to encourage your team to get over concerns about bothering other people. Persuade people to get to know one another and build up a level of trust that will allow them to pick up the phone to address an issue without being afraid. Instant messaging is another good step, but it's not a substitute for a conversation. You get the words but not the feeling; you can't pick up on the passion in someone's voice through words on a screen. However, instant messaging does allow for real-time exchange of information and is a good first step toward powerful conversations. It can help get your team back in the habit of sharing time in their daily work.

One- or Two-Step People

Leaders often encounter two types of people. One type includes those who take in and process information quickly and make quick decisions. The other type consists of those who absorb information slowly and always think they need time to sleep on it until they feel comfortable making a decision.

1 Step | · – – – Meeting · – – – |

2 Steps | – – Meeting – – | *and* | – – Meeting – – |

It is very difficult to force the two-step people to skip a step and take information in, process it, and make a decision in just one meeting. These people need extra time to go through their comfortable two-step process. It takes a little more upfront thinking on your part and a little extra time, but when your goal is to get a decision, a little extra time is worth it.

Being Consistently Different

Most of us know the Golden Rule: "Do unto others as you would have them do unto you." Unfortunately, this is not the best way to guide good communication. You don't want to communicate to others they way *you* would like it; rather, you want to do so the way *they* would like it. You must follow Tony Alessandra's Platinum Rule and "Treat others in the way *they* would like to be treated."

Successful leaders and great communicators know that communication success requires consistently different approaches. Although these leaders always convey the same message, they package those messages in ways that allow others to understand them better and faster. They adapt to others' communication styles and as a result enjoy far more effective interactions.

The following story highlights differences in communications styles, especially across cultures. Years ago, a consortium of companies—one American, one German, and one Japanese—was working on a product together. They discovered that each culture disciplined people for mistakes differently. They expressed the differences using an analogy of a hamburger.

- - - - - - - - - - -

Bun

- - - - - - - - - - -

Meat

- - - - - - - - - - -

Bun

- - - - - - - - - - -

The Americans gave you first the top bun: "How's everything going? How's the family, etc.?" Then came the meat: "You screwed up, and don't let it happen again." Last came the bottom bun: "Don't worry. John over here will help you to do it better the next time."

The Germans had no bun; you received only the meat: "You do this again, and you will be in big trouble." In fact, one German mentioned that it usually is raw meat—not even cooked.

The Japanese were the opposite; they gave you only the bun. They were so indirect that others had no idea what they did wrong. They might have gotten some ketchup or mustard, but no bun.

Your success in getting your messages across to others is often linked to how you construct the hamburger. For example, if you were talking to your boss or people higher up, would they want more meat or bun? Meat, of course; often, less is more with bosses. However, if you are communicating to someone who wants a little small talk before getting into the issue—maybe a new employee who is still getting the hang of things—starting with the meat might be too much. The person may get nervous and potentially not listen to your first few sentences or take the message to heart.

Being consistently different is about adapting your style to the one best suited to the person or persons with whom you're communicating.

Understanding Others' Perceptions

What's important to one person is not necessarily important to another. When you're leading across distances and cultures, everyone has his or her own perceptions of what is important; in many ways, leadership is about aligning these perceptions. To influence others most effectively, you need to understand the starting point of your influence: the other person's perceptions. These are the pictures in the other person's head that remind him or her of what is important—and the more you understand these pictures, the better you'll be able to influence them.

An enterprise systems project leader in a global consumer business was leading the implementation of an entire suite of systems in one of his company's international subsidiaries. This was not his first implementation, and he realized the importance of understanding people's perception of what is important. In doing any implementation, users gain something they never had and lose something they always had. However, these gains and losses are not of equal importance—and this project leader knew that getting the users' support during the implementation was tied to the way the users saw their gains and losses.

As such, the project leaders amplified the gains and focused on making the other solutions around the losses as easy to adapt as possible. They did this by investing time to understand the users' perceptions—the pictures in their minds of how everything worked and was connected—and then adapted their own communications to both recognize and manage those perceptions to their own advantage.

It is frequently more difficult to understand these perceptions when working across cultures, and the project leader understood this well. He negotiated a senior manager's support during the implementation. This senior manager acted as sort of a culture mentor, which made a big difference to delivering the results for which the project leader was responsible.

How well do you understand the pictures in your people's heads? Those pictures provide the context for everything you communicate. If employees have the wrong context, then they take the wrong meaning on board. Successful leaders know that the starting point for creating an impact with their communications is to understand the pictures in their people's head, for those perceptions color everything they hear and read.

Fair Is Not Achievable

You often hear managers say, "I just want to be fair." But as we discussed in Chapter 7, being fair is an unachievable goal because everybody has a different, and definite, opinion of what *fair* is.

So rather than focusing on trying to be fair, successful leaders focus on being *consistently different*. They know they cannot treat everybody the same way, so they treat people in a way consistent with how they're behaving, what they want to achieve, how they view themselves, and what their potential is.

They adjust their communication style to be most effective for the particular individual they are engaged with; they adjust their approach; they adjust their methods for sparking motivation. A one-size-fits-all approach will leave some team members engaged and motivated and others not.

Conversely, an unsuccessful leader will do everything the same with every employee, regardless of each one's desire to grow and contribute. Such a leader will try to give people equal time and try to motivate everybody in the same way because he thinks this is the fair approach, even if it doesn't work.

Success in leadership is about being consistently different.

You might be wondering, *"In which ways do I need to be consistently different to be more successful in leadership?"* The answer, of course, depends on your people. But you can start by understanding that people are all different. Because leadership is about influencing them, you have to find ways to influence and motivate each one—usually discovered through trial and error. But always spend your time and effort on those employees who are taking the time and effort themselves.

Reinforcing the Right Behavior

Follow-up is one of those important leadership skills that's actually more art than skill. If you follow up too closely with someone who's taking ownership of a given project, you become an irritation. Follow up too loosely with someone who's not taking ownership, and things don't get achieved on time.

Let's consider the following example. You've asked one of your people to complete something by this Friday. However, you become busy and forget to follow up with her on Friday and don't remember to do so until the following Tuesday.

What do you believe this person is thinking? First, she is probably assuming that your request wasn't all that important; even though you claimed to need the work done by Friday, you obviously didn't, or you would have asked for it then. Second, she could be thinking that whenever you ask for something in the future, she probably has two extra days to get it done.

You cannot afford to have people making these types of assumptions. The way you approach follow-up determines the behaviors you get, how much ownership employees take, and how important they feel both their work and the dates you request are.

Following up sends a signal that "this is important." Similarly, the way you do it can emphasize the importance of what you are asking your people to do. The best leaders will follow up in all different ways; they are consistently different in their follow-up and approach. They learn who needs what kind of encouragement and/or independence early on and treat those people accordingly going forward to get the best work out of them.

For instance, let's say that one leader's team members have an important meeting in another country today and the results of this meeting are crucial in making progress on a key initiative. The meeting ends at 17:00, and at 17:30 the leader sends a quick SMS text message to his team member asking, "How did the meeting go? Did we accomplish this . . . ?" Although it probably took the leader only 10 seconds to send along that SMS, the team member receives a clear signal that this initiative is important to the boss. A mere 10 seconds of investment allowed the leader to stay at the top of the team member's mind for the next two weeks.

Getting Others to Think, Feel, and Do (The Outcome of Communication) (Takeaways)

- Always focus first on the outcome of getting others to think, feel, and do.
- Adapt your style of communication to others to gain rapport and be more relevant.
- Use the power of examples and stories to bring what you say alive in others.

Your Key Reflection Questions

- What do I want the person with whom I'm speaking or meeting to think, feel, and do after this interaction?

- How well am I adapting my approach to other people's preferred communications styles?

- How am I following up and reinforcing the commitment in my people?

Part IV
Driving Performance (Enabling Team Ownership)

A successful team is one in which all members share ownership for the team's achievements. Because they own the team's achievements together, they will find a way to *work together* effectively to achieve them.

Successful leaders focus on creating the right environment, one in which all team members share the same principles and outcomes and focus so intently on achievement that they never want to disappoint their colleagues by failing to meet their commitments. Driving team performance is about getting *the team* to own the achievement.

Driving Performance (Enabling Team Ownership) Chapters

Chapter 10: Defining and Reinforcing the Principles and Outcomes

Chapter 11: Creating Positive Peer Pressure and Interdependence

Chapter 12: Playing the Game of Positive Politics (Stakeholder Relationships)

10 Defining and Reinforcing the Principles and Outcomes

In many MBA programs, group work makes up a significant part of students' grades. Unfortunately, groups often struggle to create a strong bond and working relationship—and their grades can suffer as well. In the groups that have worked together successfully, however, there can be found a few key enablers who have two characteristics. First, they're extremely achievement-focused, which guides more constructive conversations. Second, they invest in the time to discuss *how they would work together*. They lay out the key principles or ways of working that they know will help them work together more effectively.

You could call these the unwritten rules of what the team members expect from each other. These rules make clear what behaviors and support enhance the value of the group—and make it greater than the sum of the individuals in it.

The way your people work together and treat your customers is based on the culture you develop in your team. And because a culture is really a set of group behaviors, it's up to the team to both develop and maintain that culture. However, it's the leader's character and values that establish the core for a team culture. Then, the key team members both model and reinforce these values, thereby determining the culture's strength.

High-performing teams operate according to two crucial elements that create a strong ownership culture—one driven by *shared principles* and *shared outcomes*.

- - - - - - Behaviors (principles) - - - - - ➤ Results (outcomes)

Shared principles drive behaviors, and shared outcomes drive the results. Successful leaders focus on making certain principles visible and discussed within their teams: how everyone should work together, as well as the outcomes everyone is aimed at achieving. The key words here are *visibility* and *discuss*.

One project leader in a consumer business would provide a summary of the key outcomes (deliverables) for the coming week. By making these outcomes visible to everyone, there was more commitment from all to achieve their part and not let their fellow team members down. It is impossible to drive the right positive peer pressure within a team without making both key individual and team outcomes visible.

When is the last time you discussed the values or principles of your team? You can never expect people to really live value or principles if they never discuss them. Discussion of principles will always keep them both alive and relevant in your people's minds.

The visibility of outcomes encourages people to focus on achievement *together*. Leaders look at the outcomes as both *results* and *experiences*—with the customer's experience with the company being one of those key visible outcomes.

I've already cited the saying, "What is talked about, comes about," something that's true for principles as well. You can't simply call them your principles, define them, and post them on the wall. You must routinely discuss, reinforce, and live them. Successful teams do this every day.

Shared Principles or Ways of Working

To drive the right collaboration, especially across distances and cultures, you need some agreed-upon principles or ways of working.

Every country and business culture has its own ways of working; often the most important are the *unwritten rules*. These are what guide the key behaviors that affect how people collaborate with others.

Now, you cannot get everyone to behave exactly the same way, nor would you want that. However, shared principles and tactics allow team members to determine what they can expect from one another. The teams that talk through the shared expectations that matter the most will then create the most important principles or ways of working that guide the right behaviors across the team.

One of the key principles or shared expectations is around communications and the response time team members should expect from each other on their communications. Teams have set response times on e-mails, SMS messages, and the like, and that guides consistent behaviors across the team. One example is having everyone respond to e-mails within 24 hours or respond to SMS messages within 2 hours.

Shared Outcomes That Drive the Right Results

Visibility and focus on shared outcomes drives the right level of collaboration. When team members feel they own part of a collective achievement, they don't form boundaries on what is theirs versus someone else's job. Rather, they help one another do whatever it takes to achieve the team's shared outcome. The more a team shares the results, the more intense the collaboration is to make it happen.

Visibility of shared outcomes is crucial. Successful leaders find ways to highlight who owns what achievements across the team. Making outcomes visible means that people cannot hide; they *must deliver*. Leaders and teams that fail to catch poor performance early enough have likely not made these shared outcomes visible. Making goals known encourages key people to help ensure that the goals are achieved.

Participation drives ownership.

The more you foster involvement and participation within your team, the more ownership your employees will feel for their achievements and the goals of the team. And when you are working on complex projects, people are always supporting different parts of your projects. Each component is needed to accomplish the team's goals, which means that all member of the team need to feel that they are part of something bigger than their own particular role.

|---- *(their part)* ------------------------|

Even if your people's input is relatively small for a particular project or initiative, they tend to have a stronger investment in the ultimate outcome if they've participated in it. This is why smart leaders try to involve as many members of their team as possible. They encourage them to find solutions and come up with new ideas. When people see their ideas come to life, they will inherently take ownership of the end product.

How can you get your team more involved? Increased participation drives more ownership, which you can foster by establishing processes that encourage people to talk through ideas and goals together. When people get to provide their input, however small, then see how their input was used, they are immediately connected to the end result. They feel a greater sense of ownership in the initiative or outcome.

Start Discussing Right Away

Think about the meetings you currently hold with your team. How often do you get people together for an hour-long meeting in the hopes of reaching a solution to a problem, only to end up spending

45 minutes getting people's ideas and just 15 minutes discussing them? It's important to find a way to empty the ideas out of people's heads and begin discussing them as soon as possible.

| - -Input - - | - - Meeting (start discussing right away) - - |

If you're running a virtual meeting, you can prepare by asking for input ahead of time. Request that each meeting attendee come up with three to five ideas. Have them send their input via e-mail, paste them into a spreadsheet or get a Google Doc going, and quickly sort them to group similar ideas. You can then start your conference call by having everyone look over their ideas and discuss their merits. It will help people to see these ideas grouped together in categories, which may provide some hints on how some might be combined. It also gives everyone in the room a chance to share their ideas.

Odds are that the people in the room who are doing all the talking don't always have the best ideas; they're simply the most vocal. Silent individuals likely have some good ideas as well. The faster you discuss the contributions, the faster you'll be able to build on those ideas and come up with even bigger ones.

Successful leaders find a way to start discussing ideas from the very first minute. To get more out of your meetings, think about asking for input ahead of time. If you're getting the ideas out of people's heads quickly, you'll be able to begin your discussion sooner—and have stronger, better ideas as a result.

Bringing the Customer into the Conversation

You probably have different types of structures among the distances and cultures you work across. When your structure has this kind of complexity, you are bound to have differences of opinion on how to move forward. There's a simpler way to resolve these types of conflicts within the team: simply bring the customer into the conversation by asking,

What does the *customer* want?

Or better yet: *What would the customer be willing to pay for in terms of what we are proposing to do?* The unifying factor—and the thing that brings people together—is a customer, because everyone realizes that without customers, you have no business.

By asking your team to think about how the customer experience could be improved, you have a target for choosing the best option and way to move forward. If you have a strong team with diverse talents, you will always have people with different opinions on what to do. Bringing the customer into the conversation is one of the best ways to tackle this.

Defining and Reinforcing the Principles and Outcomes (Takeaways)

- Make shared outcomes visible to drive collaboration across the team.
- Shared principles drive the right behaviors across the team and the culture.
- Participation motivates ownership, so focus on making sure everyone contributes.

Your Key Reflection Questions

- How would I recognize whether my people and I were living the team's principles?

- Is everyone participating? Do I need more ways to involve everyone?

- How often do I hear the word *customer* mentioned throughout the team?

11 Creating Positive Peer Pressure and Interdependence

I've found in my experience leading international organizations that two labor-saving leadership approaches are absolutely crucial: peer pressure and interdependence.

Peer pressure drives people to perform. They don't want to let their fellow team members down, and they don't want to look bad by failing to deliver what they promised. Interdependence creates an environment where people *need* to work with each other, or their own personal success is at risk.

These two approaches drive performance and teamwork without requiring as much effort from the leader. Peer pressure requires you to make the right information on performance *visible to everyone*, whereas interdependence requires you to structure the work in such a way that people need to *effectively work with others* to achieve personal success.

People who lead successfully across distances and cultures are always seeking ways to get better performance from their team—and trying to figure out how to do it without putting in long hours. These two approaches have the power to drive more teamwork and more performance, with far less time invested.

Let's look at each in more detail.

Positive Peer Pressure

All leaders want to get enhanced performance from their teams without having to constantly drive and follow up with their people.

Which is more powerful: manager-to-employee pressure or employee-to-employee pressure? Most people believe—rightfully so—that employee-to-employee pressure is more effective. That's peer pressure. Every effective leader focuses on creating positive peer pressure to drive greater performance within the team. If encouraged and conducted in positive ways, internal competition can make employees incredibly productive.

Back in Chapter 2, you learned about the importance of *why* power for leaders: specifically, it creates pull to get things done. The other power is the leader's position, which creates a push to get things done. Now, the real power of peer pressure is as follows:

Why power `- - - - ▶` Pull your people to perform `- - - ▶` Goes up with use

Position power `- - - - ▶` Push your people to perform `- - - - ▶` Goes down with use

The more you use why power, the more your influence with each pull goes up. The more you use your position power, that is, telling people what to do because "I'm the boss," and the more you use your position to push, your power of influence in each push goes down.

Peer pressure is push without *you* needing to push.

In other words, you'll get people to perform more effectively by using peer pressure, because it actually drives *more* performance with *less* time required by the leader.

One executive in a global technology company was asked to build a regional team from existing country operations. Before, these country operations leaders reported to a local manager and were able essentially to do their own thing. When they became part of a regional team, they had to establish and use common metrics to measure their performance.

Each country's performance was reported and compared against the others. In addition, each country had its own targets based on past performance and was measured against them (green = good, yellow = close, red = far behind).

Making each country's targets and performance visible to everyone created peer pressure: no country wanted to look bad in front of the others. However, another behavior emerged as well: countries that were underperforming were getting in touch with those that *were* performing for advice on what they were doing differently. The visibility of metrics drove people to seek advice from their more successful peers.

There will always be some team members who don't want to take the level of personal ownership you want. Peer pressure can help with this by creating an environment where poor performers just can't hide. Once everyone is able to see how they're doing, they feel compelled to do more to support the team better—or they will look bad in front of their peers.

Of course, there's always the chance that one of your people doesn't care all that much about looking bad in front of peers. That's probably a sign that you should move this person out of your team. People who don't care about how others perceive their work ethic and performance usually lack both a sense of ownership and pride, something that will only hurt you as a leader every day they are on your team.

Peer pressure reveals the conflict.

Some leaders don't like conflict among their employees; they worry that they won't be able to handle it. However, peer pressure doesn't *create* conflict; it only makes visible the conflict that was already there. Successful leaders want to be able to see the conflict; only then can they do something about it.

In fact, successful leaders *search out* conflict within their teams. They know that when left alone, conflict will often fester, eventually becoming a barrier to effective communication. They also know that as conflict grows, so does the amount of time and effort it takes to get your people to work through the conflict. Therefore, as a leader, you should be strong enough to embrace the conflict in your team, as there is also stronger performance waiting for you on the other side of a resolved conflict.

You will always have conflict of some type within your team. First, it's important to know whether you can deal with this conflict in a formal meeting or whether you have to bring the individuals together in a separate meeting. Conflict between two people often extends to others within the team, so if possible, you should look first to see if you can deal with this in a team meeting. Second, if it requires a more informal meeting with just the individuals involved, it is important for them to be doing the talking and you (the leader) to just be facilitating the conversation. Although you might get pleasure from driving a solution yourself, your people will never take full ownership for a solution if it is not theirs.

Interdependence

Interdependence occurs when people need to work together with others in order to achieve personal success. You can create interdependence by establishing responsibilities or projects that require people to get their colleagues' support, making it so that they need their team members' help to achieve their own project's success.

An international leader had taken over a customer service team with people located across western Europe. He was asked to consolidate the team and put all the operations into a single location supporting all the European countries. The team was divided into six clusters of countries, He established a sense of interdependence by assigning a specific European project to each of the team's six cluster leaders. This structure ensured that each of the leaders needed the others' help to deliver their own European project. To enhance its importance in each leader's mind, the executive tied 50 percent of the leader's bonus to the potential success of the European project. Although money is not really a motivator, it *does* do a great job of providing a focus.

◄ - P - - P - - P - - Interdependence - - P - - P - - P - ►

Because each cluster leader needed his or her fellow leaders' cooperation to achieve project results, all had to find a way to get along and work together effectively, even if they didn't like each other (which they fortunately did). The cluster leaders became a "real" team and worked well together because they *had* to; their personal success was at risk if they didn't!

You can create interdependence in almost any team; it involves giving different people in your team small projects to drive on behalf of the whole team. Each person will need the help of colleagues to deliver the project, and all must therefore find an effective way to *work together*. Otherwise, personal success is at risk. Leaders end up with a double win by using this approach: you get some work done on behalf of the entire team, and you underscore the importance of teamwork.

Creating Positive Peer Pressure and Interdependence
(Takeaways)

- Peer pressure creates push without you personally having to do the pushing.
- Peer pressure makes conflict visible, so you can deal with it.
- Interdependence drives teamwork, because your people need to work together to achieve goals and find solutions.

Your Key Reflection Questions

- Have I made visible all the milestones and outcomes for my team?
- Are the metrics driving the right level of positive peer pressure for the team to perform?
- Are there any small projects that could help create interdependence within the team?

12 Playing the Game of Positive Politics (Stakeholder Relationships)

One American-based global consumer company decided to consolidate two regional business unit back-office operations into one. These two units were spread across various countries, and only the back-office operations were to be consolidated, which meant that the new consolidated organization would report to the two regional business unit managers plus the overall geographic manager. You can imagine the politics the executive of this organization encountered in reporting to *three* different bosses. Add to this the fact that the company was under tremendous cost pressures and that constant change had become the norm.

It was practically impossible for the leader of this consolidated back-office group to keep the three bosses aligned. One was always thinking differently from the others, creating real problems for the leader in his efforts to keep his message to the organization consistent. The inconsistencies were making extra work for everyone. They even prompted a few of the back-office operation's key leaders to confront the executive regarding the lack of alignment. They didn't welcome the extra work that was coming their way as a result of this unpredictability. Like it or not, if you don't play politics at your level, the people below you will often feel the impact.

Many leaders want to avoid playing politics. These are usually leaders who don't invest time to build strong stakeholder relationships, leaving their teams at a disadvantage. Although not always desirable, playing politics is important for both you *and* your team members.

When a leader cannot align goals and initiatives with other leaders across the company, that failure often translates to more complexity and more work for that *leader's people*. Over time, the leader's people will resent doing the extra work they wouldn't have to do if their boss could simply work more effectively with his peers.

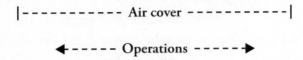

Failing to get the right alignment at your level is like asking people to fight a ground war with no air cover. And considering the organizational complexities that leading across distances and cultures often brings, providing this air cover is an absolute necessity. Otherwise, you will likely lose key team members' respect.

Whether or not you particularly enjoy playing politics, politics can be found everywhere in our lives. To lead successfully, especially across distances and cultures, you will need to play *positive politics*. Positive politics is about getting others aligned with your focus, which they won't do until you listen to *their* focus first.

Most people are familiar with the biblical story of Noah's ark. Did Noah start building the ark before or after it started raining? *Before*, of course! He knew he had to have the structure in place before he needed it to function—the same goes for you. You must build strong stakeholder relationships *before* you need them, and you have to contribute something before you can call on these connections for support. Otherwise, people will see you coming and think, "What does he want from me *now*?"

You play positive politics by *building the relationship before you need it*. Do not be the leader who gets in touch only when a problem or issue arises.

When you're seeking alignment on issues or trying to find a win-win with someone without a solid relationship already in place, achieving a worthwhile result is far more difficult. And when people scattered across the globe are not aligned on concepts, they're far less likely to achieve your outcomes with the speed and quality you demand. When leading across distances and cultures, this kind of alignment becomes one of the key enablers in achieving high performance from your team. Not only must *you* build the relationship before you need it, but you must encourage your people to do the same at their level.

The most successful leaders have a list of all stakeholders crucial to running their operations, both currently and for the next year or two. They scan this list regularly and ask themselves, "How am I doing? Am I building and maintaining relationships with these individuals?" These people know that they'll be able to move forward and achieve a win-win much faster if a solid relationship is there in the first place.

One of the best ways to build strong relationships is to ask others for advice. You're not going to them with a specific need; you just want to get their thoughts and ideas on something. When you ask others for advice, you are making them feel good (sort of stroking their ego). You learn more about them and get some great advice, too. And because you made them feel good, they often carry over that feeling to do something to help you successfully implement their advice.

Seek out one of your stakeholders this week and ask his or her advice on something.

Managing Your Stakeholder Network

Many leaders use the following method for stakeholder management. They simply classify how each stakeholder feels and acts regarding the leader's goals: positive, neutral, or negative. Then they figure out a way to move the stakeholders to where they need them to be.

| - - - Negative - - ➤ | - - - Neutral - - ➤ | - - - Positive - - - |

Negative: They are against your initiative and expressing that to others, too.

Neutral: They haven't expressed whether they are supportive or not (and maybe the goal doesn't impact their self-interest).

Positive: They have been openly supportive of your initiative and are saying so to others, too.

The most common mistake leaders make is trying to move a stakeholder from negative to positive when all they really need is for the stakeholder to be *neutral*. Smart leaders have a clear picture of their stakeholders and are constantly working on keeping these critical relationships strong. Leaders know there will always be a time when they will need the stakeholders.

One approach is to try to understand where resistance might come from and then think through how you might be able to address it. Who could help you change those negative stakeholders' minds? In what ways could you engage their help?

Do you have an analysis of your key stakeholders? When you get busy in driving the day-to-day operations of your team, you often forget about stakeholders—that is, until you need them. Good leaders, especially those leading across distances and cultures, will always keep and regularly review a list of their key stakeholders.

Culture Context for Managing the Politics

The *culture* of your team and company has a great deal to do with your *influence approach and style*. Three key dimensions help create a successful culture.

Leadership

Understanding how leadership gains its power in the company is very important. If it merely comes from the title of "boss," then you know the company will always follow exactly what the boss wants. You can also predict that you'll have to go through each link in the chain of command to get any significant change adopted.

If, however, leadership gains its power through the leader's personal ability and style, then you know that individual leaders will take more initiatives on their own—and want to make more of a difference. By persuading the most important leader to support *your* change, you often win over the other leaders, too.

Boss ◀ - - - Leadership - - - ▶ Person

So consider how your boss gains power: Is it through the position or because of the kind of person he or she is?

Communication

The way a company communicates tells you both how it will handle change and at what speed it makes change. The more direct people are, the faster they will address problems—and find solutions. The more diplomatic and afraid to offend people are, the longer they will sit on problems. As a result, you spend one meeting after another avoiding the reality of a certain situation. Communication style is one of the most important factors in understanding how you need to adapt your approach and style to gain the influence you need among team members. You need to hit the sweet spot between being too direct and being overly diplomatic:

Direct ◀ - - - Communication - - - ▶ Diplomatic

How do people communicate within your team? Are they telling it like it is, or are they always packaging the message and as a result failing to get to the point?

Change

Last, the way a company views change has an impact across everything it does, and ultimately on its focus and the choices it makes. Teams that see change as good will make an effort consistently to find and implement improved methods. Teams that operate under an "If it works, why change it?" mentality will be reluctant to do anything differently. They take a traditional view, often deciding to change something after it is too late.

New ◄ - - - Change - - - ► Tradition

Do your coworkers view change as something good to be embraced, or something bad to be avoided?

Who Has the Power?

In many large corporations, understanding who has the power is important in influencing others to support your key initiatives or changes. This is especially crucial when leading across distances and cultures, and within matrix organizations. In addition, understanding and using that power can sometimes mean the difference between success and failure.

Leaders often focus on line managers for their needed support.

Project leader or line manager?

However, large corporations have big projects that drive fundamental changes; very often, these projects' leaders have greater visibility and influence than the line managers. When leaders seek support from both groups, they build far more power to drive their key initiatives or changes.

The Importance of Peer-Influencing Skills

To play effective positive politics and create strong stakeholder relationships, a leader must possess good *peer-influencing skills*. We discussed the concept of pull and push in Chapter 2. If you'll recall, pull influence comes from the why, and push comes solely as a result of the leader's position as the boss. You obviously don't have push with your peers, because you're more or less in the same position as they are. You *have* to use the why in this case—and building the why for the peer in getting them to think, feel, and do what you want them to do (because they want to do it).

Being able to influence your peers spreads a sense of team accountability. If you fail to gain support from others, then both your personal and team productivity suffer. You have to consider how much time you require to build the strong stakeholder relationships you need, and how you do so at the same time you're running your team. This combination of your responsibilities brings us back to the lesson we learned in Chapter 1: being outcome-focused in your leadership.

If you bury yourself in trying to manage team activities, when will you find the time to build those strong stakeholder relationships you need? Successful leaders find the time to do both well. They know that only they can build influence with the most important peer relationships. However, they also know that they can use key people to help drive performance, which leaves them with more time to seek the support that will provide the air cover mentioned earlier.

◄- - - - - - -   Peer relationships   - - - - - - -►

So, how much energy do you expend building strong stakeholder (peer) relationships?

A public utility's executive leadership team was asked the following question: "For your own personal and team's success, what percentage of your focus should be on developing strong relationships and alignment with your peers, vendors, and customers, and what percentage of your focus should be on leading your team?" Most people would expect them to say 25 percent peers, vendors, and customers and 75 percent leading their team.

In fact, the answers were exactly the opposite. It was 75 percent peers, vendors, and customers and 25 percent leading the team—which, if you think about, makes perfect sense. You can get your key people's help in leading your team, but often you're the only one who can develop the strategic relationships needed to achieve the right level of influence.

Capture Their Exact Words for Future Influence

This technique is especially helpful in your communications and influence, particularly with your peers and the people above you.

Consider the following: *If you attend training, do you record the exact words the instructor is saying, or do you paraphrase most of the information?* Most people do the latter. Although that generally works in a training setting, it might not be the best approach if you are in a business meeting with people you need to influence. In that scenario, you want to try to capture their *exact words*. You want to record what they're saying in the way they express themselves, not in your paraphrased notes.

Capturing what someone else has said *verbatim* allows you to use those words in the future discussions with that person. Whether it's in an e-mail or a face-to-face meeting, you'll be speaking that person's language, and he or she will instantly get what you're saying.

This has two positive impacts.

- *It proves that you were listening* to the original message—so closely that you're able to echo it.
- It prevents the person from having to translate *your* message back into *his or her* language, thus saving communication time.

Remember, another person's words and way of saying something has more influence on others than yours.

Package Your Goals in Their Priorities

The way you package your communications regarding what you want can make all the difference when you're trying to gain support from your boss or other leaders. Everyone, even the most selfless person, is inherently focused on his or her own self-interest. Therefore, your communications are always better received when you package your own goals in terms of others' priorities. When you convey a message aimed at others' self-interest, you always get their attention. And if you can use their exact words in describing what you want within their priorities, they listen even more closely.

Deliver before Asking

When communicating with bosses or those above you, there's one habit that builds leverage with your boss like nothing else can: accomplishing something of significance *before you ask* for anything.

I heard the story of young leader who always asked his boss for some type of resource or support whenever he received a new initiative. Rather than figure out a way to deliver by using what he already had, he simply sought out more. His boss saw this habit as a weakness and started to reconsider the work he was giving to this leader. The boss began regularly giving the more challenging and visible initiatives to other leaders.

Why was the boss reacting this way? By always asking for more on the new initiatives, this young leader wasn't demonstrating any leadership ability in looking at different ways to use the resources (people and money) he already had. Because change is a constant, leadership is about constantly looking for new and innovative ways to use existing resources to do more and achieve more.

When the young leader noticed this, he questioned his boss, who responded by saying, "You need to learn to deliver first, before asking."

Intelligent leaders know that asking first puts them in a disadvantage. Your boss doesn't expect your first step in a project to be requesting additional resources or support. You have been given the assignment assuming that you would be able to balance priorities and deliver it on your own. Therefore, to create more leverage in your relationship with your boss, always *deliver before you ask.*

One last thought on positive politics: you'll never be good at or win a game in which you don't participate. Even if you don't enjoy politics, choose to play positive politics and focus on building strong business relationships—*before* you need them.

Playing the Game of Positive Politics (Stakeholder Relationships) (Takeaways)

- Build your key stakeholder relationships before you need them.

- Listen to others' focus first, and then they will be willing to listen to yours.

- You need to play positive politics in order to give your people good air cover.

Your Key Reflection Questions

- Have I identified all the key stakeholders who have an impact on my team?

- How am I doing in building and maintaining my key stakeholder relationships?

- Am I providing the right management alignment (air cover) for my team to be successful?

Part V
And Finally . . .

Reading a book is simply an activity. Now comes the important (and slightly more difficult) part: using what you have learned to alter the way you are thinking and to take new actions—that is, to change your mind-set and behavior.

Your continued self-development is crucial to advancing in your career and cultivating your potential. And the way you go about this process, along with the focus you bring to it, will make all the difference.

It starts with embracing and maintaining the right focus and then investing time to reflect on your experiences and behaviors to drive your continuous improvement. That's what we'll look at specifically in this section.

Follow-Up 1

Growing with Others' Life Experiences

In addition to advancing your team's performance, one of your top leadership priorities is to grow your people. The most successful leaders understand that motivating people to manage their own personal development is one of the keys to growing them faster. In fact, your team would be in big trouble if your people were using only the training your company provides to progress.

As Charles "Tremendous" Jones said, "You will be the same person in five years as you are today except for the people you meet and the books you read." Essentially, Jones is referring to the process of growing by way of others' life experiences. You and your people cannot experience life fast enough to grow at a pace necessary to achieve your own and your team's goals. To grow this quickly and substantially, you need to learn from the people you meet or read about.

There's a saying, "If you are the smartest person in a room, you need a new room!" Because you become like those around you, it's important to surround yourself with people who are better than you, people who will help lift you to a higher level of performance. Remember, you will always grow to the level of those around you.

And although what you experience may be new to you, it's not (always) new to others. You can learn from what others thought *and* from what they did. The books you read, the speeches you hear, the video you watch, and the conversations you have all help you learn from others. They provide examples of both successes for you to repeat and failures to avoid. It's all about applying those lessons to *your* life.

Of course, these lessons have power only if you apply them. You must also hone the ability to call on these lessons at the right time, when you need them the most. How many times have you read something in a book and thought to yourself, "That's interesting," and then just kept on reading? If you keep your thoughts at a "That's interesting" level, you never think about the action you could take from what you have learned. Applying this information is the only way to develop yourself and make changes in your life. You need to turn what you find interesting into action by asking yourself the following question when you have that aha! moment while reading:

How would I apply this to *my* life?

When you begin thinking about how you can apply what you've learned, you are seeing it in an action mode and you start storing the information in the way you would use it. You file the lesson away in your brain based on how you would *use it*, not on how you learned it. In this way, you're wiring your brain for action. The next time you have a similar experience, your brain will remind you, telling you, "Try this."

In summary, your leadership success is based on how well you and your people leverage others' life experiences and apply the messages inherent in them to your own lives.

Growing with Others' Life Experiences (Takeaways)

- Invest in yourself every day by learning from others' life experiences.
- With everything you learn, ask yourself: "How would I apply this to my life?"
- Remember that success is a team sport and that you grow faster when you learn from others.

Your Key Reflection Questions

- Consistently ask yourself as you read, listen, watch, and speak to others, How would I apply this lesson to my life?

- Is my current way of learning helping me develop my mind-set and abilities fast enough to reach my goals?

- Am I reaching out to the *right people* who can help me to develop faster?

Follow-Up 2

More of, Same as, Less of (The Power in Being Specific)

One of the best ways to move lessons into action is to use a simple framework with three columns labeled more of, same as, and less of. It's a great way to capture the new habits you need to develop (more of), those habits you need to reinforce (same as), and those habits that are not helping, the ones you can eliminate (less of).

The real power in this framework comes when you *specifically identify* the habits. Far too often, leaders list habits in general terms and then never implement them. When they are general in your mind, you don't make the link to action as fast as you need to. The power lies in getting specific.

So ask yourself, *What specifically will I do?* And then answer this: *How would* others *recognize that I'm doing it?* Greater performance is driven by what you do daily and weekly. If you do something only occasionally, it doesn't have the power to move you forward fast enough. So when you start applying the lessons from this book, be very specific about the habits you want to develop, reinforce, or replace.

- *More of (develop):* These are the things that you either should begin doing or should be doing more of to achieve the right performance level.

- *Same as (reinforce):* You are already doing these things now; you just have to remind yourself of the importance of continuing to do them.

- *Less of (replace):* These things are causing you problems, certain behaviors that prevent you from motivating your team to collaborate and take more ownership for results.

More of	Same as	Less of
1. _____	1. _____	1. _____
2. _____	2. _____	2. _____
3. _____	3. _____	3. _____

When you are more specific in what you need to take action on, you will take more action.

More of, Same as, Less of—the Power of Being Specific (Takeaways)

- The power to change comes when you get specific
- You have to develop new, reinforce current, or replace old habits
- When you are specific on action to take, you take more action

Your Key Reflection Questions

- What should I do more of, the same as, and less of to achieve more leadership success?
- What are the specific new habits I need to create?
- What are the specific habits I need to replace with new ones?

Follow-Up **3**

Daily and Weekly Reflection Guide

Reflection questions are one of the most simple and proactive tools for you to use to speed your own habit changes. Just by asking yourself a few key questions, you bring to the top of your mind the focus for which you want to change, and it drives you to reflect on the opportunities to make those changes based on your most recent behavior.

These reflection questions provide the opportunity to give yourself your own advice. It's almost like being your own coach; it forces yourself to think and bring your own best advice to the front of your mind. Last, reflection questions are a great way to remind yourself and amplify the importance to you at the same time. If you get into both the daily and weekly habit of reflection time, it will help you keep a stronger focus on the important and will drive you to develop stronger habits that will power your leadership success.

Daily Reflection Questions to Consider

- Have I been speaking in the language of achievement?
- On a scale of 1 to 10, how is my attitude today? (Remember, a 10 is just a choice!)
- How would I apply this new learning to my life?

Weekly Reflection Questions to Consider

- How was my use of pull and push this past week to get things achieved?

- How is our glue (our collaboration)? Our trust? Our information sharing? Our processes?

- How was my combination of questions and answers this past week?

Key reflection questions from each chapter are listed here:

Your Key Reflection Questions (Summary from All the Chapters)

- P: To what level are my key people feeling ownership for the team's achievement?

- C1: Have I focused all my conversations and meetings on achievement (on outcomes)?

- C2: How did I use pull and push this past week to get things achieved?

- C3: How is our glue (our collaboration)? Our trust? Our information sharing? Our processes? Do we need to take some action to improve it?

- C4: Why did I behave that way, and how could I behave better in the future?

- C5: On a scale of 1 to 10, how is my attitude today? Remember, a 10 is just a choice!

- C6: Have I protected my recovery and thinking time for the coming week?

- C7: How much of my time do I focus on developing my key people?

- C8: How was my combination of questions and answers this past week?

- C9: What do I want the person with whom I'm speaking or meeting to think, feel, and do after this interaction?

- C10: How would I recognize whether my people and I were living the team's principles?
- C11: Have I made visible all the milestones and outcomes for my team?
- C12: How am I doing in building and maintain my key stakeholder relationships?
- F1: How would I apply this new learning to my life?
- F2: What should I do more of, the same as, or less of to achieve more leadership success?
- F3: Have I defined my most important daily and weekly reflection questions?

Daily and Weekly Reflection Guide (Takeaways)

- Reflection questions bring a focus to the behaviors you want to improve.
- Reflection questions on recent behavior amplify their importance.
- Reflection questions are a great way to reinforce new behaviors.

Your Key Reflection Question

- Have I defined my most important daily and weekly reflection questions?

APPENDIX

This appendix contains a few things to help remind you of the key messages from the book and provides additional resources to help with your further leadership development. The author's biography also shares the story of his own leadership journey and experiences.

Summary of Chapter Takeaways

Resources: www.markfritzonline.com/resources

Author Biography

Summary of the Chapter Takeaways

Preface

- Your leadership success exists in proportion to your staff's ownership for achievement.

- Differences in distances and cultures are the real acid tests for leadership and situations in which you must lead outcomes.

- Strong mind-sets and habits will extend your leadership without extending your day.

Part I: Mind-set of Achievement and Collaboration

Chapter 1: Thinking and Discussing in Outcomes versus Activities

- Package all your conversations in the language of achievement; that is, speak in terms of outcomes.

- Ask your people for the milestones. Their responses reveal to you how they need to be led.

- Drive outcomes-focused meetings; you cannot afford to waste your people's time.

Chapter 2: The Ultimate Outcome Is Success (And the *Why* behind it)

- The equation of success is why > how; that is, every leader is a chief explaining officer.

- Focus on creating the conditions that enable your people to achieve success.

- Successful leaders know that action precedes inspiration, so they complete the necessary evils early in their day.

Chapter 3: Creating the Environment for Effective Collaboration

- Everything starts with trust. It is never a constant, and it needs a focus every day.

- Encourage your people to pick up the phone if they have a problem or opportunity rather than exchanging e-mails.

- Help your people find their shared common interests; this is where their conversation starters are.

Part II: Leading Yourself (Personal Ownership)

Chapter 4: Everything Starts with You Understanding You

- Your ability to understand yourself provides the foundation for you to better adapt to others.

- Distance magnifies behavior, so focus on bringing the best you each day.

- Requesting feedback from others and reflecting on your behavior is the fastest way to grow.

Chapter 5: Strengthening Your Character and Focus (Your Foundation)

- Charisma attracts people to you, but your character keeps them with you.
- Be disciplined to do what's needed when it is necessary.
- Create and maintain your focus, and force the urgent to compete with the important.

Chapter 6: Keeping Your Perspective and Balancing Your Stress

- Balance your stress with some type of recovery to keep your stress glass from always being full.
- Make your recovery and thinking time a priority that you protect.
- Plan in advance to confirm your focus and to keep your thinking ahead of your team.

Part III: Influencing Others (Enabling Personal Ownership)

Chapter 7: Investing in Your Key People (The Extension of You)

- Your key people are your team's role models when you are not there.
- Focus on and have your key people develop other team members.
- Concentrate primarily on your people's strengths and only one weakness to help use their strengths better.

Chapter 8: Delegating Outcomes and Asking Open Questions

- Delegating is the fastest way to grow your people.
- Ask more questions rather than giving answers; never save your people from thinking.
- True delegation starts when you delegate what you like to do.

Chapter 9: Getting Others to Think, Feel, and Do (The Outcome of Communication)

- Always focus first on the outcome of getting others to think, feel, and do.

- Adapt your style of communication to others to gain rapport and be more relevant.

- Use the power of examples and stories to bring what you say alive in others.

Part IV: Driving Performance (Enabling Team Ownership)

Chapter 10: Defining and Reinforcing the Principles and Outcomes

- Make shared outcomes visible to drive collaboration across the team.

- Shared principles drive the right behaviors across the team and the culture.

- Participation motivates ownership, so focus on making sure everyone contributes.

Chapter 11: Creating Positive Peer Pressure and Interdependence

- Peer pressure creates push without you personally having to do the pushing.

- Peer pressure makes conflict visible, so you can deal with it.

- Interdependence drives teamwork, because your people need to work together to achieve goals and find solutions.

Chapter 12: Playing the Game of Positive Politics (Stakeholder Relationships)

- Build your key stakeholder relationships before you need them.

- Listen to others' focus first, and then they will be willing to listen to yours.

- You need to play positive politics in order to give your people good air cover.

Part V: And Finally . . .

Follow-Up 1: Growing with Others' Life Experiences

- Invest in yourself every day by learning from others' life experiences.
- With everything you learn, ask yourself: "How would I apply this to my life?"
- Remember that success is a team sport and that you grow faster when you learn from others.

Follow-Up 2: More of, Same as, Less of (The Power in Being Specific)

- The power to change comes when you get specific
- You have to develop new, reinforce current, or replace old habits
- When you are specific on action to take, you take more action

Follow-Up 3: Daily and Weekly Reflection Guide

- Reflection questions bring a focus to the behaviors you want to improve.
- Reflection questions on recent behavior amplify their importance.
- Reflection questions are a great way to reinforce new behaviors.

RESOURCES

www.markfritzonline.com

Thank you for investing your time to read this book. My wish is that it's provided you with some ideas and insights to help you achieve even greater leadership success. I have also pulled together some resources that have been very helpful to me; if you go to www. markfritzonline.com/resources, you will find a list of recommended viewing, reading, and listening to help speed your own leadership development further.

Just a few observations from my own leadership development over the years:

- Audio books are great resources, especially if you get books that are read by the author. These authors put such passion into what they are talking about, you will undoubtedly consume the lessons in a deeper way than reading the book yourself.

- Listen to interviews of authors about their books. They usually are giving you some real gems in a way to entice you into buying their book.

- Watch or listen to leaders' interviews. They frequently use stories and examples from their experiences, and you will often learn more from one interview than you could ever learn from an entire book.

- Your development requires that you to take more action and move yourself and your team toward what you want—and in a faster way. If you already understand the concepts and why they are important, then knowing more about it is not as important as taking action. You will learn even more and in a faster way by taking action than continuing to learn more of the same thing.

My wishes are for you to achieve everything you want in leadership and family life and that you thoroughly enjoy the trip.

ABOUT THE AUTHOR

Mark is an "international," having lived in Europe, the Middle East, the Far East, and in his home country, the United States. He is married to a Japanese wife and resides in London, a city where the world comes to you, and with its air links, a city that makes it easy to go out into the world.

Mark is focused on helping leaders drive more ownership for achievement from their team, whether they are located across the country or across the world. He is an expert in the leadership mindsets and habits that drive ownership for achievement across distances and cultures, and he is a visiting professor at the IE Business School in Madrid, Spain.

Mark also speaks regularly on leading across distances and cultures and is affiliated with the global speaking bureau CSA Speakers. His popular keynote talks are Why You Never Wash a Rental Car (on leadership success using the power of ownership) and What Do Your Inbox & Calendar Say About You? (insights into how your inbox and calendar reveal the type of leader you are). He is associated with the Global Leaders in Law group and delivers seminars on leadership to general counsels throughout the world.

Mark brings the experience of an international business career with Eastman Kodak Company to his mentoring, speaking, and teaching. He has worked in various areas of the business (IT, customer service, distribution, and quality), has led Pan-European teams, and has been part of Pan-European business model developments during this time with Kodak. Early in his career, Mark led the implementation of home-grown enterprise systems in Kodak companies around the world, providing him with tremendous expertise on how business works: both top to bottom and end to end. He has worked internationally for more than 30 years, working across distances and cultures daily, and also provides business cultural coaching to executives who are moving between regions of the world.

Mark is the author of *Time to Get Started*, a compilation of the best of his Daily Thoughts found on his website at: http://markfritzonline.com, and *The Truth about Getting Things Done (Getting More Done)*, which is also available in the Chinese and Korean languages.

Mark has a Daily Thought project he started in 2005. His goal is to write 50 years' worth of thoughts (more than 18,000 thoughts), a project that's going to take some focus and energy. The why behind this project is the vision of making a difference forever. To make this vision a reality, Mark will be donating the IP (the 18,000+ daily thoughts) to a charity who can continually provide the thoughts to everyone beyond his lifetime and earn some funding for their charity projects as well. The target to complete the 50 years of thoughts is by the end of 2020. You can find each day's thought using either an iOS or Android app, which can be downloaded for free at m.markfritzonline.com.

Mark is currently looking for an international charity to become the permanent home for the daily thoughts so that his thoughts will live beyond his lifetime and make a difference forever.

INDEX